C of Red
The Beginning
of the
Calgary Flames

by

David Maiers

Contents

Chapter 1 – Early History
... page 3

Chapter 2 – Professional Hockey Returns
... page 23

Chapter 3 – A Franchise for the New South
... page 34

Chapter 4 – Enter Calgary
... page 56

Chapter 5 – The Arrival of the NHL
... page 69

Chapter 6 – Opening Night
... page 84

Chapter 7 – The Playoffs Beckon
... page 91

Chapter 8 – Who is Next?
... page 108

Chapter 9 – The Cup is Close at Hand
... page 140

– Index
... page 161

Introduction

Originally written during 2005, **C of Red** is a story about the early years of professional hockey in Calgary, Alberta including the arrival of the National Hockey League and the first season of the Calgary Flames. This book is dedicated in memory of my cousin Cam Alf who was general manager of the 1993 Manitoba Junior Hockey League champion Dauphin Kings and well-known in international hockey circles.

Special thanks to the staff of Brandon University, the Calgary Public Library and the Glenbow Museum. Thank you to the various citizens of Calgary and southern Alberta I spoke to over the course of research. Research included reading books on the early history of the city and examination of the *Calgary Herald* files at the Calgary Public Library. Calgary is a tremendous city and you made me feel welcome. Thank you.

Further thanks are extended to Mrs. Carol Densmore and Mrs. Liz Ritchie for proofreading the initial writings in 2005 that form this book.

All content within the pages of this work have been researched to the best of my abilities and with the materials at my disposal. This was an exhaustive search for material. All errors or omissions are my responsibility.

Roblin, Manitoba
September 2021

David Maiers
copyright D. Maiers 2005, 2021
all rights reserved
isbn 978-0-9737954-4-8

Chapter 1 – Early History

It is hard to believe that the cosmopolitan city of Calgary has only been in existence for just over 100 years. The city has been so much a part of Canadian sports and economic lore that it is often taken for granted as always being there. Nestled among the rolling plains of the Rocky Mountain foothills, Calgary has had a varied and rich history.

Over 10000 years ago, the advance and retreat of the massive glaciers of the Ice Age formed the undulating prairie that the city is built on. The short grasses of the region made it a particularly good habitat for the herds of thousands of buffalo that were to dominate the landscape. Native American bands of hunter-gatherers such as the Sarcee and the Blackfoot settled in the region building their lives around the movements of the buffalo. These large, powerful animals would provide the necessary means of living for these tribes, becoming the primary source of food and clothing for these indigenous people.

The native communities that resided along the Bow River and its tributaries lived undisturbed for hundreds of years. Under a land grant from King Charles the Second to his cousin Prince Rupert of the Rhine, the region to be known as Rupert's Land was formed in 1670. The grant would eventually change the way of life for the Native Americans who resided on the western great plains as this royal decree gave the fur trading Hudson Bay Company access to well over one million square miles of territory that would later form much of Western Canada and portions of the north central United States. Under provisions of the agreement all lands whose waterways drain into Hudson Bay were now open for exploitation by the prince and his business associates.

The lack of a widely forested area, which was considered ideal habitat for fur bearing animals, slowed the progress of European traders into the prairie regions. With little interest in anything outside of animals such as the beaver and the muskrat, Hudson Bay Company traders would not visit the Calgary region until the late 1700s and a somewhat permanent presence was not established by the trading firm until Old Bow Fort was constructed 40 miles west of present day Calgary during 1832. This small trading post was established with an eye to developing trade with the indigenous populations into the Rocky Mountain region but proved unsuccessful closing only two years later.

Again the aboriginal population continued to live on largely unhindered by the advance of the white man in what would become southern Alberta and contact continued to be infrequent. Then during the late 1840s a Captain John Palliser would visit the northwest United States with a native hunting party. Palliser was impressed with this great land he had visited and the Irish geographer printed a memoir of his visit that would open the eyes of British politicians to the development of the far western reaches of Rupert's Land beyond that of fur trading. The Palliser Expedition of the late 1850s would subsequently map out much of the Canadian prairies and eastern approaches to the Rocky Mountains. Although Palliser would conclude that the prairie region of Rupert's Land would be too arid for growing crops needed to support permanent settlement, the expedition would lead to an important discovery. James Hector, a geologist on the expedition, found the Kicking Horse Pass, which would later become the primary artery for expansion into the interior of British Columbia.

Other expeditions followed Palliser and that coupled with the fact American traders were beginning to travel in the southern prairie belt of Rupert's Land to trade alcohol for buffalo robes made the decision for the Hudson Bay Company to sell its large land grant to the then two year old Dominion of Canada during 1869. Shortly after this period the developments that lead to a community located at the confluence of the Bow and Elbow Rivers began.

In 1871 a gentleman by the name of Fred Kanouse set up a post to trade with the local native population. With the Hudson's Bay Company monopoly gone traders began pouring into the southern prairies largely from the United States to the south. Eventually, this interaction between the new wave of traders and the aboriginal population nearly lead to disaster. Within a matter of only a few short years the large herds of bison were almost completely slaughtered by both native and white man alike. With the buffalo herds diminished and alcoholism plus violence beginning to run rampant, the Canadian government decided to put an end to it in 1873. Through a parliamentary decree the North West Mounted Police, later to become the Royal Canadian Mounted Police, was formed to patrol the southern prairies, assert Canadian sovereignty and end the lawlessness of the traders along with the hardships facing the aboriginal people in the region.

Subsequently, the first armed force of NWMP officers arrived in southern Alberta during 1874. After establishing a presence at Fort Macleod, west of current day Lethbridge, in 1875 Inspector Ephraim Brisebois led the F Troop of the NWMP north from Fort Macleod to the junction of the Bow and Elbow Rivers to set up a permanent base of operations. Brisebois established a campsite on the west bank of the Elbow River and just south of the junction with the Bow. Following the example set by Assistant NWMP Commissioner James Macleod who had named the post at Fort Macleod, Brisebois dubbed the post he had established Fort Brisebois. Fort Brisebois sat on the south side of the Bow River with its entrance facing directly north.

Commissioner Macleod, unhappy with both

Brisebois and the name of the post, removed him from command and quickly renamed the site Fort Calgary after Calgary, Isle of Mull, Scotland during 1876. By this time the NWMP fort had in addition a relocated Hudson's Bay Company post from 40 miles west and in the area of 75 people living around the site. With that the first permanent settlement on the Bow and the Elbow Rivers had begun.

It would be the coming of the railway that would transform Calgary into what it is today. With continued fears of American encroachment into Western Canada and threats from the newly found province of British Columbia of leaving Canada, the federal government signed an agreement with the Canadian Pacific Syndicate during October 1880 to build a railway from Eastern Canada through northern Ontario, across the prairies and mountains to the Pacific Ocean. The original route for the railroad had been documented as going through Yellowhead Pass, near present day Jasper, Alberta, hundreds of miles north of Fort Calgary. Over time the routing was changed during construction of the line west from Winnipeg to a more southerly route and there were hopes Fort Calgary would be on that alignment. This was largely due in part to the discovery of Rogers Pass in the Selkirk Mountains 200 miles west of Fort Calgary by A. B. Rogers. As a result the federal charter was changed to allow the Pacific Railroad to build through the Rogers Pass area.

When the railhead reached Fort Calgary during the summer of 1883, many workers were surprised to find a bustling community of over 300 on the otherwise desolate prairie plains. As construction proceeded further west toward the Rockies, Canadian Pacific dubbed the siding set up at Fort Calgary as Siding Twenty. This to signify this was the 20th siding west of the railroad town of Medicine Hat.

Subsequently, the railroad built a small station from a boxcar and Calgary began to become an important point as a supply center for railroad construction now deep within the Rocky Mountains. By late 1884 the small center had nearly doubled in size to just over 500 people, eventually gaining official status as a town late that year. The community continued to grow as a rail line was built north from Calgary towards Edmonton and the city's population numbered just under 5000 by 1892. On January 1, 1892 the community of Calgary was anointed the title city and Canadian Pacific made Calgary an important railway terminal town by building a switching yard and locomotive service facilities in 1898. At that point the railway had firmly established its presence in the city, a role that continues today.

It was during this period of settlement and growth that hockey first began to take root in what would become the bustling city of Calgary. The first accounts of anything that resembled participation in the actions of skating and ice hockey came from the

1880s. Indeed the first published reports of skating taking place on a frozen ice surface was from 1883. During November of that year reports indicate that members of the Northwest Mounted Police were spending some of their leisure time skating on a small pond near the site of the Fort Calgary barracks. Whether these actions influenced the development of a skating rink on the nearby Elbow River is not known. However, one must assume that two gentlemen by the name of Barvis and Broderick must have been influenced somewhat by this display. This tandem was responsible for the financing and operation of this relatively small rink during the winter season of 1883/1884. Although this facility was nothing more that an area cleared of snow with the frozen Elbow River providing the ice surface it was not without its luxuries. This 140 square feet ice surface was equipped with lighting to enable skaters to enjoy skating during the evening. While the lighting system involved small lamps hung off fir trees surrounding the ice surface, the arrangement appears to have been effective. Author Will McLennan, in his highly regarded book <u>Sport in early Calgary</u>, indicated that change facilities were included for women in the form of a small wooden hut. An idea that surely appealed to the female residents of the community!

It is believed that this small facility on the Elbow can truly be called Calgary's first skating rink and its success would mean other entrepreneurs would jump into the skating rink business. Due to the mild winters and weather systems that cause the formation of warm wind patterns known as Chinooks blowing into the Calgary region from the Rocky Mountains to the west, keeping ice throughout the winter seasons was a chore.

During late 1884 what is believed to be the first covered ice surface west of Winnipeg was built by a fruit storeowner by the name of George Fraser. However, as noted above, keeping the natural ice surface in good condition in the mild winter conditions proved impractical. By the end of the 1884/1885 winter season, Fraser had a floor installed to make his rink into a facility for roller skating which could be utilized year round. While skating rinks began to become popular in Calgary the development of hockey seemed to be slow in evolving. Nothing of any formal organization of the game appears to have taken place, only on frozen ponds and rivers. It must be assumed that the operators of the first rinks in Calgary frowned upon the practice of allowing a few men swinging wooden sticks on their ice surfaces where the more lucrative thing to do was fill the rink with as many fee paying ice skaters as possible.

This attitude however, did not stop what is believed to be an unorganized game of hockey taking place at the outdoor Star Skating Rink, which was operated by Star Bakery owner Mr. F. Clayton, on Christmas Day, 1885. Eventually these games were becoming organized and by the early 1890s a league was formed in Calgary. Newspaper accounts indicate January 1893 as the first formal hockey games to take place in Calgary, the first being at the Star Rink between two teams known as the Town Boys and the Tailors. This game has been pointed to as being the first formal hockey game played in the region that would later become the province of Alberta. The Town Boys winning the contest by a score of 4-1. From that point on the development of hockey truly began to take off. Several teams were formed and organized hockey truly began to take shape in Calgary and the region.

Until that time curling had been the accepted wintertime sport or recreational skating. Indeed, there was more consideration given to constructing an indoor curling rink before a facility especially built for ice hockey was ever considered. From the 1890s forward the demand for facilities for public ice-skating and hockey continued to be dealt with by private individuals, unlike the public funding we see today.

While smaller rinks sprouted about Calgary the most important facility to date would go up in 1904 and also become home, for a time, to one of the most important figures in Calgary and Alberta hockey development. Built with financing from George Irwin, the Sherman Rink would be built at the corner of 17th Avenue and Centre Street south of the Canadian Pacific Railway line and was becoming a bustling downtown area. This facility would be the largest built in Calgary to that time. While Calgary had earned the reputation of being known as the "Sandstone City" for all the buildings built from that material in the downtown region, this arena was largely built of wood, which would prove to be its downfall.

Under Irwin's ownership this rink was originally named the Calgary Auditorium Rink. Irwin eventually sold out to Calgary theatre owner W. B. Sherman and the nickname Sherman Rink quickly became the formal name for the facility. When you are in the entertainment business a person needs to know how to promote and Sherman soon had Sherman Roller Rink painted across the exterior walls of the structure.

Ironically, the Sherman Rink was similar in many ways to the Saddledome facility built nearly eighty years later. The builders decided not a single obstructed seat should be found in the building. The overall size of the rink was 96 feet by 200 feet and the 48 foot high ceiling made it one of the largest facilities of its kind on the prairies. Curved trusses allowed for the unobstructed views and the total capacity was about 5000 people. When Sherman Rink opened it was originally built only to be a roller rink. The man responsible for making the Sherman Rink into a dual-purpose facility was Lloyd Turner.

Turner had come with his family from the east following a short period in Fort William, Ontario as both a player and manager of a hockey team. Turner would eventually become manager of the Sherman Rink and one of his first missions was to make the necessary changes to the facility to allow an ice surface to be put down over the flooring of the roller rink. During the winter months from December through March the Sherman Rink was set up with an ice surface for ice-skating and the rest of the year was in its original roller rink format. Ironically, Turner was known more for his baseball playing skills than his skills on the ice at the time. However, his organizational skills in the field of hockey were second to none.

While amateur hockey was thriving during this period in the form of small-organized leagues and later with the establishment of the Alberta Amateur Hockey Association in 1907, professional hockey where participants are paid for their play had not yet taken hold.

Further to the north in Edmonton hockey teams were battling for the Stanley Cup. The Stanley Cup was a trophy that could be competed for by simply issuing a written challenge to play for the cup to the true owners of the cup, the stewards who decided the worthiness of the opponents. The trophy itself was only a small cup of which only the top portion would be implemented into the design of the trophy presented today.

   Edmonton had launched a formal challenge late in December 1908 and the appropriately named Edmonton Hockey Club played the champion Montreal Wanderers for the small trophy. This would be the first hockey team to travel east by train to try to win the cup. This would be professional hockey in every sense of the words with the first Edmonton challenge club including some of the best players money could buy such as Lester Patrick. The Edmonton Hockey Club tried to arrest the cup from the Ottawa Senators in January 1910 however, as in their earlier adventure to Montreal fell short on the attempt.

   Perhaps it was the Edmonton Stanley Cup challenges and interest in a professional league that saw Lloyd Turner bring the first professional hockey contest to Calgary in 1913. During the spring Turner brought in two hockey teams from the Pacific Coast League to play a game at the Sherman Rink. New Westminster would go on to defeat Vancouver 10 to 8 in a much-talked about and heavily viewed contest. This would also be the first visit to Calgary of hockey in its current format of five skaters and one goalie on the ice for each team. Amateur hockey in much of Alberta at this time was played with seven players per team on the ice at any one time. During the earlier days as many as ten members of a club would be on the ice. In a sense this 1913 match was the first vestige of the modern era of hockey although seven-player hockey would continue to be the primary way of playing in Alberta well into the 1920s in many communities.

The success of the Pacific Coast League game sparked murmurs of professional hockey coming to Calgary. The flames of interest had been lit, but flames of another kind would greet Lloyd Turner and set back the development of professional hockey in the city.

On the afternoon of February 24th, 1915 fire ravaged the Sherman Rink. Newspaper accounts of the blaze indicated Turner came face to face with the flames after opening the door that separated the adjoining apartment he and his wife lived in from the arena complex. Within minutes the wooden roof was completely engulfed in flames. As with any major fire, spectators gathered near the building to watch not only it, but much of Calgary's early hockey history turn to ash. Fortunately, all inside at the time were able to escape, but items such as photographs, pennants and trophies did not. Ironically, many a rink across Canada faced the same fate causing the loss of a great deal of very early hockey heritage for the country in both places large and small.

While the Sherman Rink fire would certainly be a very memorable event in Calgary's history it did cause a void in the fledgling amateur hockey scene in the city. Turner saw fit to rectify the situation by establishing an open air rink directly across from the charred remains of the Sherman Rink. This was during the period of the then called "Great War", the First World War, and all Canadians were called upon to sacrifice from 1914 through 1918. It likely was this factor that made Mr. Sherman's decision not to rebuild the facility that once bore his name. Besides the financial situation was not likely feasible in the state of the economy geared to fueling demands of a war in Europe.

However, from tragedy and hardship can come opportunity. Following the cessation of hostilities with the end of the war on November 11th, 1918 the Canadian military informed the Calgary Exhibition Board that the large structure known as the Horse Show Building was available once again for public use.

After going three years without a large facility and smaller rinks around the city trying to fill the void, this edifice would certainly fit the bill as the replacement for the former Sherman Rink. The man chosen to oversee the refit of this former military structure was none other than Lloyd Turner. Turner saw to it that this facility should be a unique experience. British flags, which were the Canadian official standard, of various sizes were hung within the building across the ice surface and along the walls. As manager Turner would walk out on to the

220 foot by 100 foot ice surface he would be responsible for he could take comfort in the fact this would certainly be the largest ice rink Calgary had ever seen with a covered roof. The building would be called the Victoria Arena.

The conversion of the building was deemed a success as some 1200 skaters would jump on to the Victoria Arena ice surface on December 31st, 1918, New Year's Eve. As much a celebration of the city's new facility as it was a celebration of the end of four long years of warfare that saw thousands of Canadians and many southern Albertans die on the battlefields of Europe.

While Lloyd Turner was trumpeted for getting the new building quickly in order, Turner had further plans in mind. During March 1919 Turner arranged to bring in a professional hockey club in the form of the Montreal Canadiens of the National Hockey League to Calgary for an exhibition game. It was decided a team composed of the best players from Calgary's amateur ranks would be able to give this vaunted pro squad some competition for the 4000 plus people in attendance. However, the Calgarians were no match and Montreal left the city with a 12-1 victory. Of course amateurs playing against the likes of goalkeeper George Vezina, a future Hockey Hall of Fame member who would later have the NHL most valuable goaltender trophy named after him, how much of a chance did the hometown team have!

Visits by the NHL Canadiens in 1919 and the Pacific Coast League teams in 1913 had shown there was interest in the professional game. During 1921, after the success of the visits, a league dubbed the Big Four in which two clubs were based in Calgary was formed. Although the league was considered an amateur circuit as their players were not paid for their actions, neither the Calgary Tigers or Calgary Canadians played for any amateur titles available in Alberta, instead contesting for their own league prize.

From the Big Four league Lloyd Turner could see that a professional league might work in the prairie provinces. The success of the Big Four loop certainly showed that there were crowds large enough to support a professional loop. During August 1921 the Western Canadian Professional Hockey League was born and the champion of this new league would be involved in competition with the champions of the Pacific Coast and National Hockey Leagues to determine the winner of the Stanley Cup each season. The games between the champions of each league would be the forerunners of the Stanley Cup playoff format that would mesmerize television audiences decades later.

Calgary's entry into the WCPHL, the Tigers, had their shot at the Stanley Cup during the end of the 1923-24 hockey season. This would be the first time Calgary would play for the cup, which is somewhat surprising considering their northern neighbour had launched challenges two decades previous and hockey had become quite popular in the city in the intervening years throughout Alberta. However, the Tigers had a strange road to go over before having a chance at what was already becoming hockey's most sought after trophy. The Tigers beat the Regina Capitals to win the WCPHL title, then proceeded to play the champions of the Pacific Coast League, the Vancouver Maroons, who would go down to defeat. Under the agreement the three professional leagues had, the Calgary Tigers should have simply jumped on a train for the East to play the NHL winners, the Montreal Candiens. The Tigers did go, but surprisingly they had company, the Vancouver Maroons who they had just eliminated from contention for the 1924 Stanley Cup! It was then decided that both the Maroons and the Tigers would go east due to financial reasons. The more games that could be played for the Stanley Cup would result in more pay for the players was the story being reported in the media of the day.

The Maroons played the Montreal Canadiens in Montreal and were promptly beat in two games by the eastern team. The Calgary Tigers finally had their chance, although their earlier defeat of Vancouver amounted to only a bye in the first round of the playoffs to determine the champion.

The Tigers could not match the Canadiens, who

dispatched Calgary 6-1 in the first game. The spring of 1924 would see an early thaw in eastern Ontario and western Quebec, as a result ice conditions in Montreal were so poor that the second game was moved northwest to Ottawa. The change of venue would not help the Tigers as the Canadiens went on to beat Calgary 3-0 to win their second Stanley Cup championship. Many at the time felt Calgary would be back the next year, but the 1924-25 season would see the WCPHL champions, the Calgary Tigers, being defeated by the PCL champion Victoria Cougars. Unlike 1924, 1925 would see only the National Hockey League and PCL champions play for the Stanley Cup in Eastern Canada with Calgary forced to sit at home. Ironically, the Victoria team would be the last Western Canadian hockey club to challenge for a Stanley Cup for nearly sixty years as teams in the NHL would become the only ones that could challenge for the vaunted trophy beginning with the next season.

   The 1925-26 season would be the WCPHL's last. The league folded after that season and this ended the hopes of any chance for Western Canadian professional teams to challenge for the Stanley Cup. A new league in the form of the Prairie Hockey League was formed, but would only last one season. The Calgary Tigers would win the 1926-27 league title, but professional hockey in Calgary came to an end as many players went east to play in the stronger NHL as many others from across Western Canada had done.

Professional hockey all but disappeared from Calgary following the end of play with the upstart Prairie Hockey League. However, the Calgary Tigers name reappeared again for a short time during the early 1930's. The Western Canada Hockey League began play during the winter of 1932-33 featuring the Tigers and teams from traditional hockey centers such as Edmonton, Regina and Saskatoon that had formed the core of other professional loops earlier. The Tigers would go up against the Edmonton Eskimos for the league championship during the spring of 1933, but would fall short of winning it all. One thing that did hamper the playoff final of 1933 was the warm conditions that were causing problems with the natural ice found in the arenas of both Alberta cities. This would later become a primary factor in professional hockey leaving Calgary again after 1935.

Prior to the 1933-34 hockey season the name of the league was changed to the North Western Professional League as teams from Vancouver; Portland, Oregon; and Seattle, Washington joined the league. However, once again due to poor natural ice conditions in Calgary, the Calgary Tigers were forced to play all their playoff games on the road. By this time the ice conditions at "Lloyd Turner's Ice Palace", the nickname used by many Calgarians for the Victoria Arena, were becoming a nuisance. The Tigers would win the NWPL title against the

Vancouver Lions in Vancouver on artificial ice. As winners of the North West title, the Tigers were heralded as the pro hockey champions of the Pacific Coast and Western Canada.

During the next season the Tigers folded late in the season after teams from Portland and Vancouver informed league officials they would not make their trips to Calgary for league games. They deemed Calgary's North West franchise as being delinquent in meeting the costs outlined by the league bylaws for coverage of travel costs by visiting teams. There was also some concern that the natural ice in Calgary may become unplayable from the time teams further west departed by train until the scheduled time of the game in Calgary. With that the Calgary Tigers elected to sit out and professional hockey ceased to exist once more.

Chapter 2 – Professional Hockey Returns

While amateur hockey still remained popular, the professional version of the game did not resume in Calgary until the 1950s. A senior amateur loop known as the Western Canada Senior Hockey League had provided some wonderful entertainment for the city. The senior club was known as the Stampeders and competed against teams throughout Western Canada, as the name implies. By the start of the 1951-52 season three former members of the amateur association had joined the professional Pacific Coast League. These were the Calgary Stampeders, Saskatoon Quakers and Edmonton Flyers. Once again Calgary was a professional hockey city although of a minor league nature.

The Stampeders were playing their home games in the recently built Calgary Corral, a new hockey rink built on Calgary Exhibition grounds south of the Canadian Pacific tracks near downtown. The Corral was completed in 1950 and had a total capacity for over 6000 people and would be the main hockey and skating venue in the city for over thirty years.

Calgary's entry in the PCHL enjoyed success in both league and playoff action. By the time the 1953-53 season had rolled around the Stampeders, affiliates of the Chicago Blackhawks minor league system, had become a powerhouse in the PCHL, which was eventually renamed the Western Hockey League with the inclusion of a franchise in Winnipeg, Manitoba. The Stampeders had their most successful season to date that season.

The Stampeders beat the Vancouver Canucks in four straight games in the best of seven Western Hockey League final to that title. Then the club began a best of nine series with the Quebec Aces of the American Hockey League for the Edinburgh Cup, which was the trophy for hockey supremacy in the top tier of the minor leagues in North America. George Imlach, who would become better known by his nickname "Punch" over the years, coached the Aces.

The Stampeders were coached by Frank Currie, who had one of the best teams he had ever claimed to coach under his command. The star of the team was a gentleman by the name of "Slippery" Sid Finney who was tied as the top goal scorer of the Stampeders. Finney was noted for his talent of notching goals with a very quick shot. Finney was the top paid player on the team at $8000 per season, which would have been a very high salary for a minor pro player during that period, but very low by today's standards. By comparison a registered nurse at the time would be only making about $1700 per year during the same period of the mid-1950s.

Currie, Finney and the rest of the Stampeders would go on to beat the Quebec Aces to win the Edinburgh Cup with the final game being played at the Corral to a capacity crowd of well over 6000. The city would erupt in a massive celebration and this would be the first professional hockey championship of a national nature to be celebrated in the western city.

The Stampeders went on to have other great seasons in the Western Hockey League, but would not come close to replicating their two championship titles from 1954. During the 1958 and 1959 playoff runs the Stampeders made the WHL finals, but went down to defeat at the hands of the Vancouver Canucks and Seattle Totems respectively, losing both best of seven finals with four straight losses.

By the 1962-63 season the love affair Calgary had enjoyed with the Stampeders and the WHL was nearly over, or as far as the owners of the Stampeders were concerned, the Calgary Stampede and Exhibition board of directors. Board members were concerned with the rising costs of supporting a minor league team and there were also concerns raised that the Chicago Blackhawks under Tommy Ivan were not willing to provide the support the Stampeders would need to continue operations. The decision was made to sit out the 1963-64 season and subsequently the following season as well. Once again the light had been turned off with fans of the professional game waiting for a small spark to re-ignite the flames of interest.

While the mid-1960s would once again mark the end

of professional hockey at the minor league level in Calgary, decisions being made in offices and conference rooms thousands of miles away would come to influence the future of hockey in the city. The National Hockey League of the 1960s was the "Original Six", although the name is a misnomer. In fact only one of the six NHL franchises then playing was actually among the original franchises playing with the league when it was created in November 1917, that club being the Montreal Canadiens.

Since that time hockey had become Canada's game, although the national sport was officially listed as lacrosse. While lacrosse had a strong following in portions of Canada, primarily in the east, thousands across the nation were playing hockey. Sport in Canada was hockey and hundreds of thousands of people would gather every Saturday evening during the winter and spring to watch Canadian Broadcasting Corporation's Hockey Night in Canada. Television was still a very new medium with many broadcasting stations not even being past their tenth birthday by the mid-1960s. For most Canadian hockey fans you had your choice of the Montreal Canadiens or the Toronto Maple Leafs to cheer for or one of the four American based franchises consisting of Detroit, Boston, Chicago and New York. The six teams were the highest tier of professional hockey at that time and there was no other alternative.

NHL teams at this time were largely dependant on

gate receipts for their revenues. The days of pro replica jerseys, baseball hats and video games were still far off in the future. For the ownership groups of the teams, the league was the perfect business. Simply fill the buildings and count the money. The league was essentially an all cash business, an entrepreneur's dream! Although the actual figures may never be known, all the owners were considered to have done very well even with franchises such as the Boston Bruins who were often at the bottom of the standings each season throughout the 1950s and into the 1960s.

However, the buzzword of the 1960s was "television". In the United States television was seen as a way of maximizing the financial investment in a team. Major League Baseball was the first professional sport to embrace the medium and baseball ownership reaped the rewards. During the 1960s professional football was also beginning its love affair with the National and American Football Leagues having games beamed into homes across the United States. The US television market was a lucrative one and advertisers were lined up to spend dollars for sports to place their product within games.

The NHL could see this and the league knew it would need a television contract in order to expand its revenue streams. Expansion was seen as a way of obtaining that goal. Not only could revenue be generated from a television contract with an American network, but also there were fees for new franchises that could be added to the bottom line.

In order to bring about all this, the NHL announced its first major expansion in league history that would take the NHL game to non-traditional markets. Overnight the NHL doubled in size from its base of six teams to a complement of twelve. The Pittsburgh Penguins, Philadelphia Flyers, St. Louis Blues, and the Minnesota North Stars joined the NHL for the 1967-68 season along with two Californian entrants, the Los Angeles Kings and the Oakland Seals. This expansion was followed with another in time for the 1970-71 season, which would see the first new Canadian entry, the Vancouver Canucks and the Buffalo Sabres added.

Hockey purists were dismayed with the expansions citing the fact the new NHL of fourteen teams was diluted. Players who would have been minor leaguers only five or six seasons before were now being called upon to be the top line players on the expansion clubs. Others harkened back to the days when each NHL game was looked forward to featuring contests such as Gordie Howe and the Red Wings versus Bobby Hull and the Blackhawks or Jean Beliveau and the Canadiens. Now these games were being replaced in the schedule with lackluster entries such as the Oakland franchise made up of a mix of aging veterans past their prime and young recruits who in the daily writings of some hockey scribes needed more time in the minor leagues before earning the right to be in the NHL.

The reason for expansion was the ever-elusive contract with one of the major television networks in the United States. With teams now spread throughout the western states and into areas such as the upper Midwest and Pennsylvania, the NHL thought the multi-million dollar contract from an ABC, CBS or NBC would only be a matter of time. Unfortunately, that contract would not arrive following the expansion; instead expansion may have opened the door, unwittingly, to competition.

While the prosperity following the years post World War Two had fueled a great deal of economic expansion throughout North America, the 1960s were beginning to see centers in Western Canada become larger and stronger. Cities such as Winnipeg, Edmonton and Calgary were growing substantially due to a booming farm economy and the discoveries and exploitation of natural resources ranging from nickel to natural gas. Western Canada was quickly becoming a place where a person with a few dollars in his pocket, a hard work ethic and a bit of luck could enjoy a great deal of financial success. So it was not much of a surprise when Western Canadians would come to the forefront in attempt to launch a rival hockey league to compete with the expanded NHL.

The worst nightmare for the NHL owners arrived on the scene on July 10, 1971. That would be the day two Californians with little knowledge about the game of ice hockey would file the necessary articles of incorporation for the World Hockey Association in the state of Delaware. Dennis Murphy, a former general manager in the American Basketball Association, and Gary Davidson, a practicing lawyer and one of the founders of the ABA which was a rival to the National Basketball Association, had decided that hockey and the NHL in particular was missing markets that had a demand to be filled. Soon Murphy and Davidson began to make contact with some influential characters in the form of Bill Hunter from Edmonton, Ben Hatskin of Winnipeg and Calgary's Bob Brownridge. All three men were successful businessmen in their respective centers and had been involved in hockey team ownership at the junior level. Brownridge had even won an Allan Cup amateur championship in 1946 as a member of the Calgary Stampeders during his hockey playing career.

With the financial backing of this Western Canadian triumvirate, the World Hockey Association was initially proposed to be a ten team league with ownership groups set up in Western Canada plus Miami; Dayton, Ohio; Chicago; St. Paul, Minnesota; San Francisco; Los Angeles; and New York City.

The WHA made no bones about the fact they would likely stock their franchises with players from NHL teams. Few believed the WHA owners could pull off such signings, as the league only existed on paper. The only thing the WHA seemed to have going for it was an endless stream of press conferences and press releases. Without any hockey players it would certainly be hard to start a season let alone a league!

Whether NHL ownership underestimated the financial resources Hunter, Hatskin and company had at their disposal or had decided players would not give up their careers with their prestigious league is hard to determine. Then in February 1972 the WHA threat became quite real, and the decision of a young future superstar with the Toronto Maple Leafs made headlines. Bernie Parent was being looked at as a beacon by the WHA to other NHL players wanting to know if the new league would truly exist. Parent had been Toronto's number one goaltender and was being backed up by veteran goalie icon Jacques Plante. Parent had been unhappy with a controversial trade that had sent him from the Philadelphia Flyers to the Maple Leafs. Parent appeared to be Toronto's goaltender of the future, so it was with surprise that Parent had climbed aboard a plane for Miami to announce that he would be leaving the Maple Leafs to play with the Miami Screaming Eagles of the WHA for the 1972-73 hockey season.

This announcement would give the league credibility and the fledgling league continued to chase down its prime prospect, Bobby Hull. There was even open speculation in the pages of the number one sports magazine, Sports Illustrated, dedicating a front cover and coverage of the WHA's pursuit of the "Golden Jet". Few dared to believe that such a superstar such as Hull with his booming slapshot and gregarious nature, which was a marketable quantity for the NHL, would be allowed to leave or even consider an offer from the upstart league that had never played a game. However, Hull was unhappy with the way the Chicago Blackhawks had dealt with him and felt underpaid for the revenue he had generated for the team and the league during his career. By the time Chicago management and the Wirtz family, the owners of the Blackhawks franchise, reacted to the WHA overtures Hull had been receiving, he had made up his mind to leave.

On July 27, 1972 Bobby Hull did what had been unthinkable, he took his all out skating style and slapshot for the more lucrative playing surfaces of the World Hockey Association. Hull would receive a cheque for $1 million from the WHA owners in St. Paul, Minnesota then would fly on to Winnipeg to sign the contract Ben Hatskin had offered him to be a Winnipeg Jet probably for the rest of his hockey playing days. With his signature hockey would change forever. Hull was now hockey's first million dollar man.

Soon other NHL players began jumping ship for the WHA. The league had gained credibility with the

Parent announcement and became a reality with the Hull signing. Unfortunately, Calgary would not make the curtain call for the league debut in October 1972. Bob Brownridge, an influential member in the Alberta oil patch with Bow Valley Industries, pulled out of his WHA commitment due to health reasons. Along with Brownridge went Calgary's hope of a WHA franchise. What could have been a crucial blow to the start of the league was soon forgotten with the appearance of Hull in Winnipeg.

Chapter 3 – A Franchise for the New South

Ironically, the NHL sought expansion once again in 1972 while the WHA continued to make plans. Mere weeks before Hull left, the NHL announced their third expansion in five years. On June 6th, 1972 the NHL admitted the New York Islanders and the Atlanta Flames into the league making the NHL a sixteen team loop. Atlanta and Georgia were not exactly traditional hockey centers, but the city was becoming the regional capital of the "New South". It's economy was flourishing and it would be during this period that entrepreneurs such as Ted Turner would begin to emerge from "Hotlanta" to become dominant in the future course of North American and world commerce. Atlanta was also headquarters for Coca-Cola, a global giant that was only getting bigger.

While Atlanta may not have made sense from a hockey purists standpoint it made economic sense for the league. Another market for use in getting that lucrative television contract that continued to elude the league and a city with deep pockets that might want to purchase tickets. Tom Cousins would be the principal owner of the franchise and had become a successful entrepreneur in dealings with the real estate market now booming in the Deep South.

A name the team contest was held resulting in the name Flames being picked. During the American Civil War federal forces lead by General Tecumseh

Sherman marched through the city in 1864 while routing Confederate forces. Sherman ordered the city burned down as a message to the southern rebels that would become one of the many horrible defining moments of this brutal war. However, following the cessation of hostilities in 1865 Atlanta would be rebuilt to its former glory, rising from the ashes. With this event being one of the city's most notable period of history, the name seemed quite appropriate and had a history attached to it like no other franchise name in any sport.

The Atlanta Flames would enter their first season in 1972-73 with Bernie Geoffrion as head coach. This former Montreal Canadien great had earned the nickname "Boom Boom" for his quick shot and stellar goal totals. The general manager was Cliff Fletcher, who had recently left the expansion St. Louis Blues as assistant coach.

The Flames were like the other expansion clubs upon entry to the NHL, a mix of veterans and young players, most with either their best seasons ahead of or behind them. In some cases neither scenario would apply. As with most of the new franchises enthusiasm was high in the beginning and the first season at the recently built arena complex called the Omni in downtown Atlanta was usually home to decent crowds within its cavernous, circular interior. Hockey might be able to make it in the hot south after all.

As the Flames sizzled in the US southeast, Calgary remained without a professional hockey team while Edmonton and Winnipeg had enjoyed a full season of WHA action. The high price of oil coupled with an energy crisis during the early 1970s would see Calgary grow more prominent and become capital of the Alberta oil boom. It seemed every week brought about a major announcement of new construction within the city limits. New buildings had been going up since the mid-1960s, slowly changing the city skyline. Calgary was a center on the move and a city that probably could have worked within the WHA framework, but no serious bidders had come forward to pursue a franchise since Bob Brownridge pulled out. However, this was to be expected, as the WHA teams seemed to always be on the move.

Only the two original Western Canadian teams, the Alberta (later Edmonton) Oilers and the Winnipeg Jets, seemed rock solid in ownership and stability. The club Bernie Parent was to play for, the Miami Screaming Eagles, never played a single game and instead Parent would take over a $100000 pay cut to play with the Philadelphia Blazers for one season before returning to the NHL. This was regular fare for many players and franchises competing in the league.

Ironically, it would be the Blazers that would eventually bring the WHA to Calgary. After unsuccessful stays in Philadelphia and Vancouver as the Blazers, team owner and Vancouver entrepreneur Jim Pattison decided to take this franchise to Calgary. The team was renamed the Calgary Cowboys to reflect the western tradition of the city. However, the Cowboys only played two seasons in Calgary at the Corral on the Stampede Grounds.

During the first season in the city, 1975-76, the team did very well recording 41 wins and four ties over an 80 game regular season schedule and defeated the Quebec Nordiques in the first round of the WHA playoffs before being defeated by the Winnipeg Jets who would eventually become the AVCO Cup champions.

Although the franchise made a very good first impression, the team was reportedly in the red $500000 from its first season in the city. After a poor performance and poor attendance during the following season, the Calgary Cowboys folded. After spending time in three different cities over five seasons the Blazers/Cowboys, one of the original charter members of the league, was done in 1977.

The WHA-NHL feud of the 1970's was radically changing the face of professional ice hockey. Beginning with the Hull departure from the Blackhawks, salaries escalated, as did operating costs for the franchises in both leagues. Soon players and their agents were involved in bidding wars to gain a better salary. Dissatisfaction with an offer simply meant going to another franchise in the rival league to get what was wanted.

The large American network television contracts that fueled baseball and football in the United States never materialized from the NHL expansions or competition with the WHA. The game was still largely a "take the money at the gate" operation as it had been since the inception of the professional game and Canadian television contracts would never deliver the funds the team owners would eventually require to pay their rising costs.

The NHL was not immune to the traveling franchise syndrome as the expansion Oakland Seals moved subsequently becoming the Cleveland Barons. The Kansas City Scouts would be uprooted and moved off to become the Colorado Rockies. If the fans did not show up, a hockey franchise was in trouble regardless of the league affiliation or professional caliber of play.

For all the problems and benefits that came from the rivalry between the two leagues it was clear that only one could survive. The NHL decided to cease its battle with the WHA due in large part to the softening of the league's leadership with the arrival of John Ziegler as president of the league in 1977. Ziegler would take over from Clarence Campbell who had opposed any union between the WHA and the NHL. Ziegler recognized the advantage of bringing the better positioned franchises of the WHA into the NHL, further expansion along with the fees involved.

After paying $6 million each in franchise fees the Winnipeg Jets, Quebec Nordiques, Hartford Whalers and Edmonton Oilers were admitted to the NHL in time for the 1979-80 season. These four survivors had hung on long enough and the WHA folded as a professional sports league following the AVCO Cup championship final during the spring of 1979 between Edmonton and Winnipeg.

Calgary appeared to be on the outside looking in once again. There had been some hopes in Calgary that if the WHA Cowboys could hang on long enough Calgary could become one of the teams lucky enough to gain entry in a merger with the NHL. Unfortunately, Calgary only had the Corral as a facility to offer and it would certainly have to be expanded to a minimum of at least 15000 seats that was being required of the WHA franchises that gained entry. The Cowboys very rarely filled the 6500 seat Corral even one third full so there were concerns on how much demand there was for professional hockey.

With all things considered the prospects that a NHL team would be coming to Calgary seemed more remote than ever before. Although the city had doubled in population since the 1950s, the lack of a large arena complex seemed to be a major stumbling block.

Thousands of miles to the southeast the Atlanta Flames were in trouble in the Deep South. The team was losing money, substantial amounts of it. The Flames did not make the playoffs during their inaugural season of 1972-73, finishing second last in the NHL's Western Division with 65 points. Only the hapless California Golden Seals were worse that season. The following season saw the Flames rise to fourth in the West, which was largely made of expansion clubs with the exception of the Chicago Blackhawks. The Flames would later succumb to the eventual Stanley Cup champions, the Philadelphia Flyers, during the 1974 playoffs.

A fourth round of NHL expansion prior to the 1974-75 season would see more additions in the form of the Kansas City Scouts and Washington Capitals. Now an eighteen team league, Atlanta was moved with Philadelphia and the two New York franchises, the Islanders and Rangers, into the new Patrick Division named in honour of Lester Patrick.

Under this new format Atlanta would break the .500 win percentage mark that season with an 83 point campaign, but would still finish last in the four team division, probably the toughest in the league. Unfortunately, the best season in the Flames short history was not good enough to make the playoffs as only the division winner plus second and third place teams were allowed into the Stanley Cup playoffs under the new realignment format. Ironically, Fred Creighton replaced coach Bernie Geoffrion, who was having his best season to date, nearly three quarters of the way through the regular season while having a winning record!

Under Creighton's leadership the Flames would not fall below .500 over the next four seasons and would make the playoffs. But, success in the leagues second season would not come Atlanta's way. Due to goals for and against in 1975-76, the team finished the regular season paired up with the Los Angeles Kings for a first round match only to be dispatched 2-0 in the recently adopted best of three preliminary round format.

The next season Atlanta finished at the break even point with 34 wins, 34 losses and 12 ties for another third place finish and a playoff berth in the 1977 playoffs. Once again Atlanta squared off with the L.A. Kings and superstar Marcel Dionne, the league's second leading scorer behind Guy Lafleur with 53 goals and 122 points. While the Flames would win their first and only playoff game to date during this series, L.A. dumped the Atlanta crew two games to one. The subsequent playoff year would see Detroit turf the team during post-season action in straight sets during 1978.

The belief that Atlanta was a poor team was an incorrect assumption. The franchise had its stars, but could not seem to pull things together during the short preliminary series that made the NHL playoffs somewhat more unpredictable. During the 1978-79 regular season Atlanta had become the third highest scoring team in the league behind the New York Islanders 358 goals and the Montreal Canadiens 337 goals. Atlanta's 327 goals were achieved largely with the assistance of career years from forwards Bob MacMillan and Guy Chouinard. MacMillan and Chouinard would finish fifth and sixth in league scoring with 108 and 107 points respectively. They were in good company as the top four scorers included future Hall of Fame selections Bryan Trottier, Marcel Dionne, Guy Lafleur and Mike Bossy. The seventh place player was another Hall of Famer, Islanders defenseman Denis Potvin.

The Atlanta Flames looked to have turned the corner. The team had an entertaining product on the ice and looked poised to become one of the contenders for the Stanley Cup. The 78-79 Flames had their best season in seven years of existence in the hot and humid southern United States. Coach Creighton had slowly brought the franchise along and it looked like Atlanta was ready to take the next step, a playoff round victory.

The first round matchup with the Toronto Maple Leafs looked good for Atlanta that year. The Leafs had also been a team on the rise during the 1970s that never seemed to achieve greatness. With players such as Borje Salming, Darryl Sittler, Lanny McDonald and Dave "Tiger" Williams the Leafs had the tools to be a contender. However the Leafs had dropped in the standings from 97 points during the 77-78 season to only 81 the following year. This looked like an opportunity for Atlanta, but once again the best of three preliminary round was not favourable to the southern club. Toronto would beat Atlanta in a two game sweep.

Fred Creighton would not return to the bench for the next season and was replaced by a longtime American Hockey League coach from the Montreal farm system. Al MacNeil had won a Stanley Cup with the Montreal Canadiens in 1971 under what could be considered somewhat controversial circumstances. MacNeil had benched Canadiens star Henri Richard, the younger brother of legendary Maurice "the Rocket" Richard, an icon of French-Canadian hockey. Henri was nicknamed "the Pocket Rocket" and was a skilled forward, with lithe quickness and as one of the elder statesmen on the 70-71 Canadiens, looked upon as a team leader. Richard had his name on the Stanley Cup nine times from the time of Montreal's five cup dynasty in the late 1950s through back to back title victories twice during the 1960s.

During the 1971 Stanley Cup final versus Chicago, MacNeil benched Richard for game five of the series. Richard fumed in the Montreal press that MacNeil did not know how to coach and was an incompetent bench boss. These were highly charged political times in Quebec and Canada. The country had just pulled through the FLQ crisis that saw militant Quebec separatists kidnap a British diplomat and a Canadian politician. During this period the Canadian government under Prime Minister Pierre Trudeau enacted the War Measures Act, which amounted to martial law being imposed in order to restore order and capture the terrorists. These were pivotal times for the early separatist movement and the Richard benching was being used in the media as a political weapon. French language commentators used this incident to show that English Canadians, with MacNeil as their representative, did not know how to treat French Canadians correctly and obviously did not care. It is amazing to consider that a move that was made to better the Canadiens chance at winning in a tight playoff series, Richard had slumped somewhat during the series and MacNeil felt a change in the lineup was needed, had been construed as an indication of something that was bigger than hockey itself.

With all the outside pressure applied MacNeil had no choice but to return Richard back to the ice for the following two games. In the seventh and deciding game Henri Richard scored the tying and game winning goals to give Montreal the Stanley Cup once again. Richard seemed to be putting a stamp on the accusations flung at MacNeil with this performance. This put Al MacNeil in a rare spot, a coach of the

Stanley Cup champions who would have to be removed due to popular opinion. The Canadiens organization dealt with the matter in a professional manner making MacNeil head coach and general manager of the Nova Scotia Voyageurs from where the team had promoted him to his NHL job, Montreal's top notch farm club. What had been a move designed to win a game had cost MacNeil his job in the NHL. Years later Henri Richard would say he would have called any coach, regardless of background, incompetent for his benching.

Certainly Allister Wences MacNeil deserved a better fate, but the native of Sydney, Nova Scotia made the best of his situation. The following hockey season, after the controversy over Richard, MacNeil went on to lead the Voyageurs on to the 1972 American Hockey League championship. The Nova Scotia Voyageurs never finished below .500 with MacNeil at the helm and went on to win back to back league titles in 1976 and 1977. As player-coach for the Voyageurs during the 1969-70 season and head coach during six seasons from 1971 through 1977, MacNeil amassed over 300 victories and a winning percentage of .646 in the American Hockey League, impressive credentials for anyone at any level of hockey.

In Atlanta MacNeil inherited a team that looked to be a vibrant contender for the upcoming 1979-80 NHL season. Atlanta appeared to be a contender that consisted of the toughness of Willi Plett, drafted by the team 80th overall in 1975, and Curt Bennett; the scoring prowess of Guy Chouinard, Bob MacMillan and 1975 Calder Trophy winner Eric Vail. As well there was a decent goaltending duo in the form of Dan Bouchard and Pat Riggin. With an experienced coach, who was a winner everywhere he went, the possibility of success appeared real.

While the team looked to be solid on the ice and behind the bench, there were problems off the ice financially. Although the club had outdrew its Omni cohabitant, the Atlanta Hawks of the National Basketball Association, during several periods throughout the 1970s the team was in trouble. One estimate had the Flames losing $2.7 million during the 1978-79 season with the chance the team could lose a further $3 million during the 1979-80 season. There were rumours around the city that team owner Tom Cousins had also been having some problems in the real estate market and this further added to speculation that the NHL was on shaky footing in Atlanta. As a result hockey insiders were beginning to circulate rumours that Cousins was looking for a way out of his ownership of the Flames franchise. By the spring of 1980 those rumours had reached Calgary, Alberta.

There was much speculation in the Calgary newspapers that the Flames might find a home in "Cowtown" as the NHL regular season moved into its final weeks. While the rumours of new ownership and/or the team being moved to Western Canada went on, the Flames still needed to play hockey and win games to get in to the playoffs. Some hockey scribes felt that a good playoff run would be all that would be required by the franchise to turn things around. Others felt that new ownership, with the team still based at the downtown Omni in Atlanta, could be the solution to the financial woes.

Atlanta heading into the 1980s was much more than just civil war folklore and Doc Pemberton's Coca-Cola. The city had a bustling airport that was the main operational hub for Delta Airlines. Three interstates crossed through the city making it an excellent location for commerce in the southeast United States. With a population of around 2 million, many transplanted citizens from centers in the northern United States were looking for employment in this revitalized "New South". Hockey might still succeed with the right person at the helm and the correct business formula. However, those same theories were the ones used when the NHL awarded Atlanta a franchise in 1972!

The Flames did everything they could to gain more interest during the last weeks of the 1979-80 season. The team brought in Olympic gold medallist Jim Craig, the goaltender who had just days before backstopped the "Miracle on Ice" United States hockey team at the 1980 Olympics in Lake Placid, New York. Versus the lowly Colorado Rockies at the

Omni, Craig started in a 4-1 win for the Flames and his debut also brought a much needed sellout to the Omni for the team. There was some hope by fans that Craig could perform more miracles, but he would record two losses and a tie in his next starts. Craig was playing at a time when the franchise needed victories on the ice for their run at a playoff spot, not publicity and this was adding to further problems in the team's dressing room.

Bill Clement, a rugged centerman who would later go on to become a highly regarded commentator on American NHL telecasts, sounded off in the papers following Craig's departure from the team and became a vocal leader for the players in their side of the problems facing the team. Craig had been diagnosed as having suffered from exhaustion and was prescribed a period of rest in Fort Lauderdale, Florida by the Flames physician. Clement indicated in an interview that Craig was not good enough to start and that the signing was more a marketing ploy than anything associated with helping the franchise to the playoffs.

However, the Craig signing and arrival was only part of the problems facing the Flames. With constant scrutiny in the media and road trips to NHL centers bringing even more questions from curious reporters, the Flames players were now under a large microscope and were being prodded for even more information. Rumours of earlier financial problems began to appear in the media. In the same interview that Bill Clement asserted his feelings on the goaltending situation, he went on further revealing how bad things had been for the franchise even in its earliest days.

Clement had been a member of the Philadelphia Flyers Stanley Cup winning teams during their 1974 and 1975 championship runs. After a short one year stint in Washington with the Capitals, Clement was dealt to Atlanta for the 1976-77 season. The Flames were very much an upstart club still trying to find their NHL footing when Clement arrived. To his surprise he found a team on the verge of collapse. Clement and other members of the Flames gave up a portion of their salary to the team in order to keep the club afloat. According to Clement, the players purchased $30000 in season tickets to help Atlanta finish the season and management indicated that a new group would refinance the franchise. However, that would not happen.

As players began to vent, empty seats seemed to multiply at home games. Besides the Jim Craig inspired second "Miracle on Ice" sellout, most of Atlanta's dwindling fan support was evaporating under a cloud of confusion about the future of hockey in the city. Day to day the Atlanta newspapers and television sportscasts were filled with rumours of a possible move or new ownership group with no names revealed. Possible destinations included the state of New Jersey, where the Meadowlands Arena was seen as a good location for a NHL tenant in a more traditional hockey marketplace. However, the other name that had continually popped up was Calgary.

Regardless of the rumour, it was clear that there was one thing the Flames fans and players had in common, disregard for the current management of the team. Owner Tom Cousins and team president Bob Kent were slowly becoming the attraction for much of the hatred brewing over the troubled franchise between those two parties, ownership and the players. Bill Clement also let a reporter know that he had played his three seasons in Atlanta with little contact with Cousins and suggested that Kent was not a hockey fan.

While the barbs flew in the press during the closing days of the 79-80 campaign, the Flames continued to battle for playoff positioning. Under Al MacNeil and amidst all the distractions the season had brought, the Flames finished in the middle of the pack with a record of 83 points at the conclusion of the 80 game regular season. This put them in fourth in the Patrick Division behind the always tough Philadelphia Flyers, the surging New York Islanders and the 1979 Stanley Cup runners-up, the New York Rangers. This made the Patrick Division one of the toughest in the NHL. Considering all the turmoil and the tough opposition a fourth place finish could not have been considered bad.

   With the recent addition of the WHA clubs, the NHL had once again grown in size and the playoff format also changed for the 1980 playoffs. The previous format had been developed for the 1975 playoffs involving a preliminary round consisting of second and third place teams in each division doing battle and the four division leaders getting byes into the next round. This amounted to twelve clubs being allowed into the Stanley Cup tournament out of the eighteen that existed at the time. A minor change was made for the 1978 playoffs, but only twelve teams were still permitted to pass. Now with a 21 team league it was decided sixteen teams would be allowed to compete for the Stanley Cup. The NHL officials decided that the four division winners would get berths automatically as in the previous playoff format along with the top twelve non-divisional winners. This would amount to a total of sixteen franchises in the tournament with the number one seed playing the sixteenth, second playing fifteenth and so on down the line. Rather than limiting a team along conference or divisional lines this gave hockey fans a tremendous opportunity to see unique match ups. Some hockey fans that enjoyed the playoff rounds of the 1970s and early 1980s have felt the pairings by overall rankings provided the most interesting and intriguing match ups.

   Atlanta's opponent for the first round best of five

would be their Patrick Division rival, the New York Rangers. The Rangers had morphed from being a group of underachievers throughout the mid-1970s to facing the dynastic Montreal Canadiens in the 1979 final. Unable to stop the Canadiens juggernaut, the Rangers fell in five games as Montreal won their fourth consecutive Stanley Cup. With Phil Esposito as the team leader and soul of the Rangers, they were a team to be taken seriously although they had slipped somewhat in the standings from the previous year.

On the eve of this series players were still being bombarded with questions. Would the team move to Dallas-Ft. Worth or the swamps of New Jersey? What does your wife think of a possible move to Calgary? The questions were more consistent and soon the games were not the primary concern, only what venue would the Flames play at next season. Fans and reporters had also picked up on a new brochure the Omni was presenting for upcoming events. Surprisingly, there was no listing of Atlanta Flames home games for the upcoming 1980-81 NHL regular season. With the Flames not listed, the rumour mill went into overdrive in mid-April as the Stanley Cup playoffs progressed.

Coming into their best of five series with the New York Rangers, Atlanta seemed to have some factors in their favour. The Flames seemed to rise to the occasion versus the Broadway blue shirts at Madison Square Gardens. The club had been unbeaten at MSG since March 1977 in regular season play and number one goaltender Dan Bouchard had been unbeaten in his last eight starts at the historic facility. However, the Flames fire would be dimmed by the Rangers 33 seconds into the first overtime period of game one. The Rangers had scored midway through the third period to tie the Flames 1-1 and game tying goal scorer Steve Vickers struck again with his second in the extra frame over a sprawling Dan Bouchard.

As the series continued the overriding story was not the performance on the ice, but the speculation of the club's future off of it. The on ice action and off ice turmoil finally collided during the first intermission of game two at MSG. General Manager Cliff Fletcher walked into the Flames dressing room and announced that if the team did not improve its performance and win the series they would only be five periods away from moving to Calgary with two more losses in the best of five series. The comment survived beyond the dressing room making the sports pages in Calgary and other NHL centers. It would be the first public confirmation of the Flames leaving for Western Canada. Fletcher had made it clear to his team that if they lost they would move and if they won they might remain in Atlanta. However, his words did not get the response he had hoped, as the Flames could not pick up their game for the final two periods. Thoughts of new homes and new schools may have clouded their ability to come back as the Rangers won 5-1 to take a commanding 2-0 series lead.

While the threat was the talk of the town in Calgary it had confirmed Atlanta hockey fans worst fears. It was ironic that the usually quiet and dignified Fletcher would spark the final playoff victory and only the second postseason win for the team in its eight season. The words were not lost on Eric Vail, Atlanta's 1975 NHL Rookie of the Year. Vail told reporters that the players wanted the franchise to stay and succeed in Atlanta and they fully understood a playoff series defeat would mean the end for hockey in the city. Vail and his mates would respond in game three at the Omni.

As the Flames burst out onto the ice amid the cheering from 11495 fans they did so with confidence, but the crowd itself was troubling. Most NHL playoff matches would draw far more than the 11000 plus patrons at the Omni that night and the facility had seating for over 15000 fans. What might turn out to be the NHL's last stand in the southern United States had not attracted the attention one thought it might. However, the Flames would not disappoint those that did show up as they would go on to a 4-2 victory with Vail scoring two goals. It would be only the second playoff win for the franchise.

The Flames would not be able to mount a comeback to win the series. The fourth game, also played at the Omni, woud be the last in Atlanta for the Flames and the last game for the Atlanta based franchise. The

Rangers dashed hopes of a victory early when former WHA Winnipeg Jet Anders Hedberg, Dan Talafous and Ed Hospodar tallied singles within the first seven minutes of the first period. The Rangers did not look back and went on to win 5-2. The 12103 in attendance went home having witnessed a piece of hockey history on April 12th, 1980, the end of the NHL's experiment in the southeast United States.

Chapter 4 – Enter Calgary

The Flames season was over, but the rumours continued. It seemed every person with some available funds and interested in becoming a hockey team owner was rumoured to be a candidate to buy the club. The suitors for the Flames were finally identified as being the Seaman brothers of Calgary based Bow Valley Industries. Darryl and Byron Seaman, nicknamed Doc and B.J. among the Calgary business community respectively, had earned their wealth in the oil patch and were being identified as the front-runners for the franchise purchase. Both brothers had been known to speak with Tom Cousins and Doc Seaman had visited Atlanta and resigned his position on Calgary mayor Ross Alger's policy committee looking into a proposal for a new arena, among other facilities, in preparation for a Winter Olympic Games bid. As well, at the behest of team owner Cousins, Flames president Bob Kent had been to Calgary speaking with both members of the city hall and board members of the Calgary Stampede and Exhibition Board that controlled the city's Corral Arena.

While the Seaman's were designated the number one buyers for the club, other names such as Edmonton Oilers owner Peter Pocklington popped up, as well as companies such Labatt's, as suitors for the club. All this rampant talk about the new owners really began to fly after Cousins let it be known the team was truly for sale after the Flames elimination from the playoffs. Now it seemed only a matter of time before a deal would be announced.

Atlanta would not be the only team to lose money in the NHL, they appeared to be the only one moving. The Colorado Rockies, St. Louis Blues, Chicago Black Hawks, Quebec Nordiques, Hartford Whalers, Los Angeles Kings, Pittsburgh Penguins, Washington Capitals and the Flames all lost money during the 1979-80 season. The Rockies were reportedly the only other team besides Atlanta to lose over $2 million during the season, eventually their future would become murky too. Ironically, only one of the nine money losers was a Canadian franchise, the Quebec Nordiques. Only the New York Rangers bested the Edmonton Oilers $6.139 million in gate receipts. By comparison it appeared the NHL's Canadian entities were in good financial shape. This also fueled the speculation that Calgary was where the Flames would end up.

Then another viable offer appeared during the first week of May 1980. It was a dramatic offer that could only have been delivered better by a man in a white cowboy hat on a white horse. The person who would play the part of the cowboy was actor Glenn Ford. On Thursday May 1st, 1980, Ford's agent Lloyd Zeiderman notified Tom Cousins that his client would like to purchase the franchise with the explicit guarantee the team remains in the southern city. This event finally made the ongoing "who will buy the Flames" debate more public as both Ford and Cousins went directly to the media with comments on the offer.

Ford indicated he had a warm spot in his heart for Atlanta as he had acted in the region and had many friends in the city. He also indicated the booming economy Atlanta was experiencing and that the franchise leaving the area did not make any sense. During telephone interviews Ford said he could and would match the offer the Seaman brothers had offered for the franchise, which was being reported as being around $14 million.

Glenn Ford was best known for playing roles in cowboy westerns that were a big part of Hollywood fare during the 1950s and 1960s, his financial holdings were quite diverse from the money he earned acting. Ford had been successful in investing in cattle ranching and raising quarter horses. There were two strange things about this offer. One was Ford appeared to be the only serious bidder besides the reported offer from Calgary to come forward, although the papers were filled with speculation on others. The other was Ford was originally born and raised in Canada.

Glenn Ford was born in the community of Portneuf, Quebec, 35 miles west of Quebec City. His given name was Gwllyn Samuel Newton Ford, but he took the shortened name Glenn Ford after his father's hometown of Glenford, Quebec. His father Newton Ford was a Canadian Pacific Railway conductor who had played some semi-professional hockey with the Quebec Bulldogs. Newton Ford moved his family to Santa Monica, California after taking an early retirement from his railroad career and since then his son would make it big in the Hollywood movie scene. Now the little boy from small town Canada who had loved the Montreal Canadiens as a child and had grown up to be voted the number one box office star for 1958 by the Motion Picture Herald, a show business paper, was now standing in the way of Calgary's NHL dream.

However, one man did not have much faith in the offer. Unfortunately he would be key to a deal. Tom Cousins did not believe that Ford's agent Lloyd Zeiderman was serious with his initial inquiry. Cousins suggested to the Associated Press that he hoped the offer was not a hoax as it might give false hope to the hockey fans in Atlanta that the team would not move. What might have triggered Cousins reaction was Zeiderman's assertion that if another deal was presented Cousins should proceed. Team president Bob Kent also seemed somewhat unconvinced in his interviews with the press, but Zeiderman's request to see the teams financial paperwork was granted.

One theory was that this was a publicity stunt for

one of Hollywood's older leading men. As the days went on neither Tom Cousins or Bob Kent issued statements that suggested the Ford deal had not been formally presented other than a plethora of press releases and interviews with the actor. Those in Calgary were not enamored with the Ford offer. The leading *Calgary Herald* sports columnist, Larry Wood, even suggested that he loved Ford and his movies as a youngster, but he should simply "butt out" in his May 5th column.

Once again what should have been a very private business deal was fodder for the press and hockey fans and was beginning to look like a theatrical production starring the leading man of 1958! Would the Flames move to Calgary? Would they stay in Atlanta? A move to New Jersey? But the story continued to take more turns.

After pouring over the nine years worth of Flames financial records, Glenn Ford pulled out of the "does anyone want this franchise" sweepstakes. The red ink that was all over the last few seasons at the Omni was too much of a warning of the future the franchise would continue to face if it stayed in the city. With Ford out of the picture it appeared the Seaman family finally had their NHL franchise for Calgary. The viability of the Flames remaining in the south ended on May 8th when Ford's agent announced publicly that an Atlanta based team would likely lose a substantial amount of money for at least the next two or three seasons because of the state of contracts surrounding the team's operations. It was now a certainty that no further suitors would come forth to save the team and it would move somewhere. However, Ford's exit also allowed an opening to another interesting character.

So it finally appeared that the Flames were in the hands of the Seaman brothers and Calgary had their NHL franchise. During an interview on May 8th, Edmonton Oilers owner Peter Pocklington offered some inside information to the media indicating he had been in touch with Darryl Seaman and that the deal to move the club to Alberta was nearly completed. Outside of Pocklington's words it seemed a gag order had been put on Atlanta Flames employees and the Seaman family. Phone calls from media members were not returned or taken and the only material fit to print was speculation. This lead to the assumption a deal was being finalized and an announcement would be due shortly. The Seaman's looked to be the new owners, but looks can be deceiving. The brothers would find a startling development when they opened their copies of the May 15th *Calgary Herald*. The banner headline reading "Now it's Skalbania fanning the Flames".

By the spring of 1980 Nelson Skalbania had become a bit of a mythical moneyman in the mold of a Canadian version of Donald Trump. This 42 year old Vancouver real estate developer, who was born and raised in the small community of Wilkie, Saskatchewan, had a few years earlier made headlines in the sports field for being the person who brought a teenage hockey phenom by the name of Wayne Gretzky into the world of professional hockey. For all his impressive wheeling and dealing in the sports arena and the real estate market, hockey fans in Calgary were becoming a little concerned that Skalbania might ruin a move of the Flames to their city.

Tom Cousins and Skalbania held secret meetings prior to word finally leaking out in the press. Both men were heavily involved in their real estate empires and had reportedly done business before in that marketplace. Sources close to both men felt that this deal looked to be close to happening. There were rumours that former Winnipeg Jets owner Ben Hatskin and Edmonton Oilers founder Bill Hunter were behind Skalbania's entry as all three had relationships stemming back to their days in the World Hockey Association.

Hatskin denied any real interest in buying the team, but admitted to meeting with Skalbania over the issue publicly. Hunter, it later was revealed, was trying to buy his own NHL franchise and move it to Saskatoon, Saskatchewan with the Flames being one of the possible teams on his list.

An outside owner such as Skalbania, who resided in

Vancouver, was something that Calgary City Hall had not counted on if the team did come to the city. Calgary was engaged in the process of negotiating financing with the provincial and federal governments to finance a new arena in an effort to secure the winning Canadian bid for the 1988 Winter Olympics that would be decided during 1981. The 6500 seat Corral would not be suitable for such an event and an 18000 seat facility was being proposed to be built for the event. Having a year round tenant in the form of a NHL franchise guaranteed a use and operating revenue for such a structure once the Olympics were over.

An absentee owner could cause problems for the city and their proposed complex as far as deciding what was best for Calgary. Then there was a concern that Skalbania would simply buy the team from Cousins only to turn around and resell it. With a new arena expected in a few years time, Skalbania could walk away with a few more million dollars more than what he paid for the franchise. In reality a new arena for the Olympics would put money in his pocket and the ownership circus might resurface at a time the city might be concentrating on the Olympic event. Calgary might also lose their franchise on resale with the next stop possibly being Dallas or New Jersey? Skalbania had been noted for turning around assets quickly for fast profits. Many were not looking at a NHL team under his control in Calgary very favourably.

Skalbania entering the fray was an interesting concept. Not only had he owned the Indianapolis Racers of the defunct World Hockey Association during the late 1970s, but he had Alberta hockey ties having been an investor in the Oilers and co-owned the team for a time with Peter Pocklington prior to assuming control of the Racers. Many had forgotten Skalbania had been largely responsible for allowing the opportunity for NHL hockey to exist in Alberta's capital. With million dollar losses in Indianapolis staring him in the face Skalbania exited the hockey market prior to the merger of the WHA and the NHL. He only recently had returned to the hockey market purchasing the New Westminster Bruins of the junior Western Hockey League circuit for his daughter Rozanda to run. This deal being closed as the rumours of the Atlanta Flames demise in the south began gaining steam.

Besides Skalbania and the Seaman brothers there appeared to be no other bidders for the franchise. London, Ontario based Labatt Breweries, one of Canada's and North America's largest brewers, was said to be interested. There also appeared to be interest from a Saskatchewan group, later learned to be lead by Bill Hunter, and it was also believed that Coca-Cola might be interested in being the saviour that would keep the Flames in Atlanta. In the end Skalbania did as he had done before in his business dealings, he won although he may be accused of prematurely celebrating the deal.

On Friday May 16th, 1980, after weeks of speculation, CFCN radio in Calgary broke a story of Nelson Skalbania admitting he had completed the deal to buy the Flames with an eye to moving them to Calgary. This story was the result of a researcher for CTV networks investigative current affairs shows W5 doing a feature on Skalbania and his business empire. During a rare phone interview during the period of Flames speculation, it was reported the millionaire said he had completed the arrangements with owner Tom Cousins to buy the team. According to the report, broken by CFCN's Russ Peake and picked up by almost every news outlet in Canada later that day, two brothers by the names of Butch and Gus Harvey from Edmonton helped bankroll the Skalbania deal. The report went further and stated that both men had contributed to a $16 million payment wired to Cousins as he was in desperate need of financial help due to problems with his other business operations. The Harvey's were known to be involved in real estate, but little more was known other than the CFCN report indicated they financed two thirds of the purported deal.

What the report did do was put buzz on the streets of Calgary and more pressure on all parties involved in completing a deal. While Flames president Bob Kent came out the next day denying the deal had been consummated, he did finally admit that Cousins had flown to Vancouver earlier in May after meeting the Seaman brothers in Calgary. Kent also denied the story that Cousins business holdings were in dire need of an immediate financial injection. He also indicated he had no knowledge of a wire transfer between the two parties and with a sum of money that size he would have been notified.

The Seaman brothers seemed somewhat annoyed and stunned at this recent news. After two months of very secretive negotiations and revealing little publicly, in walked a rogue figure to take their dream away. Byron Seaman told interviewers that Tom Cousins knew what their offer was and what they could do financially to secure the team. He also went on to explain that the only person who knew the real situation of the sale of the team was Cousins and they would wait to hear from him.

In the meantime Molson, Canada's other nationally known brewer, had already negotiated deals separately with both Skalbania and the Seaman brothers in anticipation of a Flames purchase. Molson representative Don Henderson confirmed a multi-million dollar agreement had been reached with Skalbania with only a few minor glitches to overcome. As far as the Seaman brothers were concerned Molson made no confirmation although local media had reported that arrangement as well. But Molson officials were remaining cautious with Henderson stating that it was unusual for his company to state a business deal prior to a final decision pending on another beyond their control.

Byron Seaman once again vented in the media suggesting that this prolonged business discussion, rumours, untrue statements and new investors might be a way for the sale price to be increased. Seaman told *Calgary Herald* columnist Larry Wood in an exclusive that their position had not changed from their first generous offer. Seaman also put down the speculation their offer was more than $14 million, but not the $16 million some had reported. He also concluded that it seemed as though someone wanted to continue pushing the price up with all the confusion.

Finally on Friday May 23rd, 1980 all the weeks of speculation ended. In a conference room in Atlanta, team owner Tom Cousins walked into a room full of media and made the following announcement, "It is with mixed emotions that I announce the completion of negotiations for the sale of the team." Skalbania had his NHL hockey team, the third professional club he would be involved in. At the press conference lead by Skalbania in Calgary he revealed that he had looked at the downtrodden Colorado Rockies prior to getting involved with the Atlanta purchase. However, the Rockies had stumbling blocks such as a television contract to cancel and a requirement of a vote of 100% acceptance by NHL board of governors to move the franchise.

In Atlanta Cousins denied a bidding war had taken place. Skalbania went further on to identify problem areas with the Flames deal and why it had taken so long, in the process becoming a public mess. First a lease needed to be arranged with the Calgary Exhibition and Stampede Board to utilize the Corral for games. The lease was negotiated right up to the time Skalbania finally wired Cousins the money for the club, Skalbania insisting that if a deal could not be arranged for the arena he would have likely moved the team to Saskatchewan to play in Regina or Saskatoon until a facility became available in Calgary. He even jokingly suggested his birthplace of Wilkie might have been a suitable location for the team should the Corral not have been available!

Chapter 5 – The Arrival of the NHL

One thing for certain the Flames were now Calgary's team and immediately the people of the city were drawn to their new team. Hockey fans purchased over 2000 of the team's 20 game season ticket packages at the Calgary Exhibition offices at Stampede Park within minutes after the press conference that announced the sale. Skalbania's ownership group, which included Calgary businessmen Norman Green and former Canadian Football League great Normie Kwong, had set up operations under the name Calgary Hockey Club Incorporated and was making available about 15000 season ticket packages that would enable fans to see 20 of the 40 home dates scheduled for the Corral. One reason the season ticket packages were split was due to the cost of the tickets, which were the highest in the league due to the small facility they would play in. Another was the opportunity to buy a seat as there would be little chance any single game tickets would be available during the season, especially with the rush to buy season tickets.

With Calgary having to play in the 6500 seat Corral and space available for another 1000 in standing room, the Calgary Hockey Club doubled the ticket price found in other NHL arenas to give the team the same opportunity at revenues teams in 15000 seat facilities would enjoy. An average single game ticket price for a game in 1980 was about $7 to $10 in most

NHL markets, in Calgary the price broke down to $21 each with the purchase of a season ticket package.

While the Atlanta Flames were now going to call Calgary home, many were uncertain what they would be called or what the team would look like. A name the team contest was held with a spot being located on the application for season tickets for the name. However, many people in a rush to get their submission in quickly did not fill out a choice for a name. Normie Kwong headed the five person "name the team committee" and decided to have a drop off box for entries set up at the Calgary Inn downtown and the suggestions rolled in!

Names such as the Calgary Arrows; Calgary Broncos; Calgary Derrickmen; and Calgary Peigans (an Alberta aboriginal tribe) made up some of the entries. Skalbania was enamoured with a plan to simply add a flaming letter C next to the flaming letter A that was already on the Flames jerseys. Skalbania felt this would be a natural, the A for Alberta and the C for Calgary. However, when he told some of his people the idea they laughed. As a result the name the team contest went ahead.

As early as May 8th, Larry Wood of the *Calgary Herald* unveiled two creations of artwork by Calgary resident Kevin Lasalle. Lasalle designed two different logos. One for a Calgary Flames name showing a hockey stick with a gas flame coming from the blade of the stick and the word Flames underneath. The other was for a Calgary Arrows name with Arrows spelled out across a large letter C made into the shape of an arrowhead. Each letter forming the word Arrows also bore an arrowhead appearance.

Ultimately the Calgary Hockey Club would become the Calgary Flames with a flaming C replacing the original A as the team crest. The team would keep the same design of red, yellow and white as the team colours.

With Calgary rejoicing over the arrival of their NHL franchise Atlanta fans felt left out in the southern heat. A Save Our Flames campaign failed and chairperson Dr. Bud Kennedy accused the Flames ownership group of mismanaging the franchise the entire time the team was in Atlanta. Kennedy asserted the notion that the Flames did very little to try to stimulate interest in hockey in the city and failed miserably to promote much needed ticket sales. Kennedy's group had even gone so far as to design a new business plan for the team and a new television contract, possibly with Ted Turner's WTBS, that would have increased broadcast revenues from the existing $250000 to $700000.

Flames players were also having some misgivings about the team moving to Calgary. There they faced a higher cost of living in the midst of a booming

Alberta oil economy. Bill Clement owned a large home in an Atlanta suburb valued at $110000 and doubted he could find a similar place in his new location for that price. However, as with other players, he did admit that moving to a more enthusiastic hockey market might do wonders for the club.

Young defenseman Brad Marsh, a veteran of only two NHL seasons, was ready to go north. He told the media he could be ready within two hours notice to leave Atlanta having only his van and a piece of stereo equipment to worry about.

Willi Plett, the pounding forward who had won the 1977 Calder Trophy as NHL Rookie of the Year, told reporters on a trip to Calgary to scout out what he was getting into, that it would be a great opportunity for the franchise to start over in a more positive environment. Dan Bouchard, who accompanied Plett on his journey, had suggested earlier that he would prefer staying in Atlanta. After being in Calgary only one day Bouchard seemed to accept the prospect of playing in the city as a welcome change. Although he conceded he would not be able to enjoy the same benefits he had in the Atlanta area Bouchard seemed pleased which was quite something for a player who was often dubbed as being "moody".

Probably the most interesting figure of the Atlanta Flames was Gary Unger. Unger is most often remembered for his playing time with the St. Louis Blues and was probably the most popular player in the franchise's history. Unger was noted around the league for his combination of toughness and skill as well as his blonde golden hair streaming behind him as he blazed up the ice.

Unger had begun his NHL career as a member of the Toronto Maple Leafs during the 1967-68 season at the age of 19. As a young prospect his ice time was quite limited on the defending Stanley Cup Champions that still bore many of the veterans from their 1967 triumph. Unger was dealt to Detroit where he eventually blossomed into a star with a 42 goal campaign during the 1969-70 season. With his ample blonde hair and good looks he was dubbed the "Golden Boy" by fans and the media in the Motor City. A falling out between a newly appointed former university coach by the name of Ned Harknesss and the team saw the end for Unger in Detroit. Both Unger and others were traded away by the Red Wings after Harkness was elevated to general manager of the troubled club. Unger was sent to St. Louis with Wayne Connelly in exchange for Tim Ecclestone and Red Berenson during February 1971.

While in St. Louis Unger not only became the most popular Blue he also snapped off a string of eight consecutive 30 goal seasons, a franchise record that was not equaled until Brett Hull tied the mark during the 1990s. Unger's best hockey would be played during his eight and a third seasons in St. Louis. However, a nightmare also occurred that would mar his stay in the city.

Gary Unger held a barbeque for his teammates at his 200 acre ranch just outside of Gray Summit, Missouri on the Sunday of a warm Memorial Day weekend. Blues defenseman Bob Gassoff and his wife would attend the festivities. While riding a motorcycle just outside Unger's property, Gassoff would be hit by a car and killed on a winding road that lead to the estate. It was an enormous tragedy for the Blues and the families involved. On October 1st, 1977 the Blues held a ceremony to retire Gassoff's number three jersey and dedicated the 1977-78 season to his memory. Gassoff's number would be the first retired by the Blues organization. With this terrible tragedy behind him, Unger left St. Louis for the Atlanta Flames for the 1979-80 season. While with Atlanta Unger became good friends with Paul Henderson, the hero of the 1972 Soviet-Canada hockey series, who happened to be playing in his only season with the Flames after a couple of years with the WHA and the nearby Birmingham Bulls.

Unger looked forward to the move to Calgary, as it was his hometown. Gary Unger told interviewer Steve Simmons of the *Calgary Herald* that he would not have minded playing a couple more years in Atlanta before retiring, but Calgary was the next best thing. Unger was now the fifteenth leading goal scorer in NHL history with 394 goals and although his first season in Atlanta would be his worst statistically since his first in the league. Unger agreed with assertion that Atlanta was not the best place to play hockey with its hot humid weather patterns. He went on to say that he enjoyed playing road games in Los Angeles and that it was one of his favourite cities, but he did not want to play there for the same reason as Atlanta.

Unger was looking north as a place to revitalize his career. This was the man who had earned the title as "the NHL's Ironman", setting a record for playing the most consecutive games in league history including eight full seasons with St. Louis and a then record 79 game season during the 1970-71 campaign where he split time with Detroit and the Blues. His streak ended in Atlanta at 914 consecutive games played in a strange twist. While in St. Louis for a road game, coach Al MacNeil sat Unger on the bench for most of the game. As fans and his teammates realized that Unger's streak was in jeopardy they began urging MacNeil to put Unger out on the ice in what was a lopsided game. MacNeil ignored the pleas and the streak ended, Unger's jersey not seeing a drop of sweat. The coach would later tell the media that he was the one running the team not the St. Louis fans.

With the move largely accepted by all the Flames players there was still some concern about the facility their home games would be played in. The Corral had been in use since the 1950s and would be the smallest arena in the NHL. Rookie defenseman Paul Reinhart knew the Corral well having attended the Canadian Olympic team training camp there during the fall of 1979. His time in the building was a large factor in his finally signing a pro contract with the Flames versus remaining with the Olympic program that was based in Calgary. Reinhart at one time said that he would not want to move to Calgary if that was the building the team would play in. Within days of the announcement that Tom Cousins had worked out a deal to sell the team, Reinhart softened his stance. Reinhart feeling that the move would finally make the Flames winners.

Cliff Fletcher, whose future with the organization was openly speculated upon during the ongoing negotiations, thought the Corral would be an excellent place to play. The Flames were a relatively large team and a small building with a small ice surface would certainly be an asset. Fletcher was excited at the prospect that this little rink would become part of the intimidation in playing the Flames on the road.

The Corral was now the only thing in the way of the Skalbania deal being approved by the NHL Board of Governors. However, that approval would only be a formality. Calgary having a franchise was being viewed as an opportunity for the NHL. Creating a natural rivalry between Calgary and the Edmonton Oilers would help strengthen the western half of the league. As well eastern teams on road trips to Western Canada could include a fourth date on their travel schedule along with Winnipeg, Edmonton and Vancouver. Western teams also had another club to play with less demanding travel. Having a seventh NHL franchise in Canada also further strengthened the overall Canadian market. Calgary's city council was attempting to rectify the arena problem having hearings then approving and receiving funding from the provincial and federal governments for what would become the Saddledome. In a matter of a few seasons the Flames would have a wonderful new facility to play in, the Corral would only be a stopgap measure.

With the sale out of the way and the team officially in Calgary the work began to assemble the 1980-81 edition of what would become the Calgary Flames. There were no changes in the day-to-day hands on management team. Fletcher remained general manager, David Poile would be his assistant and Al MacNeil would be head coach. Assistant coach Tim Ecclestone decided to remain in Atlanta and did not follow the team to Calgary. This left the assistant to MacNeil open and Pierre Page was hired as his replacement.

Page was not very well known in professional hockey circles, but he certainly gained prominence in university hockey in Eastern Canada. Page turned the hockey program at Dalhousie University in Halifax,

Nova Scotia into one of the best university level programs in Canada by the end of the 1970s winning a regional championship in 1979, the first for the school in 60 years. Page had professional experience prior to his position at Dalhousie as a physical education professor having worked in the Montreal Canadiens farm organization. Prior to accepting the Dalhousie job, Page spent time as Al MacNeil's assistant with the Nova Scotia Voyageurs where he worked with a number of players who would later become pivotal in Montreal's Stanley Cup successes of the 1970's.

With management in place and a new team trainer in the form of Jim Murray, the newly founded Flames were ready for training camp. Calgary brought 58 players into training camp, which was held at the Max Bell Centre. Many were members of the team's farm club, the Birmingham Bulls; others were eager draft picks trying to catch on with either team.

The Flames swung a handful of deals over the summer that would see team captain Jean Pronovost shipped east to the Washington Capitals and Garry Unger sent south to the Los Angeles Kings. Ironically, Unger had earlier said he would not like to play in a city such as Los Angeles due to the warm weather as it was not conducive to focus on hockey!

These changes opened up some spots on the forward lines for those wanting them. One player being looked upon to step up was Earl Ingarfield Jr. Ingarfield came from an interesting background. Earl Sr. was a good player for the New York Rangers, Pittsburgh Penguins and Oakland Seals while his son grew up. The younger Ingarfeld was never drafted and had to fight hard to get on a NHL roster after a junior career with the Lethbridge Broncos. Ingarfeld was signed as a free agent by Atlanta and was sent to Birmingham in 1979.

Another player being looked at positively with hope for the future was a 20 year old, 6 foot 2 inch forward from Renfrew, Ontario. Jim Peplinski was big, strong and could both score and back check. He was drafted in the fourth round by Atlanta after spending time with the Toronto Marlboros junior team. Peplinski would survive training camp and stick with the Flames becoming a center on the fourth forward line.

Overall the Flames had an interesting mix of stars, journeymen players, rookies and veterans. The club also possessed a mix of toughness, a holdover from the days of chasing the Philadelphia Flyers in their division, and skill. Kent Nilsson, once a star player with the Winnipeg Jets during their WHA days, was to be one of the leaders on offence next to guys like Guy Chouinard, Bob MacMillan, Eric Vail and Don Lever, who was a former longtime Vancouver Canuck. Willi Plett and Ken Houston, noted for a scrap in the mid-1970's that saw him break Flyer Dave Schultz's jaw, brought strength up front.

On defense 22 year old Brad Marsh not only lead that segment of the club, but was awarded the captain's "C" by general manager Fletcher and coach MacNeil just prior to the start of the regular season. No. 22 would become the second youngest captain in the NHL and would replace the departed Pronovost as leader. Incidentally, Pronovost's new team, Washington, had the youngest captain in the NHL with Ryan Walter.

Marsh was married to Tom Cousins' daughter Caroline who would remain the only member of the family still with direct ties to the Flames franchise in Calgary. Marsh made up for his lack of speed and finesse by working hard to play positional hockey and tie the opposition up around the net. As a result, in a short time with the Flames, he had become known as the hardest working player on the team. Often he would tell the media he needed to play hard all the time to make up for his lack of skills.

Other notables on defense were men such as Bob Murdoch, a very cerebral player with a background that included a degree from the University of Waterloo, and Paul Reinhart who had the second highest point total for rookie defensemen behind Ray Bourque during the 79-80 season. Pekka Rautakallio from Pori, Finland, was being likened to the New York Islanders Stefan Persson in his speed and play making ability.

During the 1979-80 season the Atlanta Flames finished in the middle of the pack in the NHL and finished ninth in the league. The predictions for the Calgary version of the club ranged from a prediction of a twelfth place finish in the league to a very optimistic sixth place finish. Both the media and the new Calgary fans had very little to go on other than pure optimism. This was the big league making its debut in a booming western city known for its own do what it takes attitude.

Overall the Flames looked to be a good mix of young and old, but many wondered how the franchise would fair in their new digs in Cowtown. The team had the opportunity to become a legitimate Stanley Cup contender with rabid hockey fans behind them. With all games sold out at the Corral before the team had fully arrived in the city, the old rink certainly would be noisy!

For those who could not get in the Corral the new Flames could be listened to on radio or watched at home on television. CHQR radio would broadcast all 40 home dates as well as the 40 road games. The broadcast team included play-by-play man Bart Dailley with Peter Maher and Doug Barkley joining him in the booth.

Local TV station CFAC, a CTV affiliate, would use the talents of longtime Calgary sportscaster Ed

Whalen, who was well known in many Western Canadian markets as host of Stu Hart's Stampede Wrestling television programs. Ending each show with his line, "In the meantime and in between time that's it another edition of Stampede Wrestling. Bye-bye now." Former NHL player Gary Dornhoefer would be "Wailing" Whalen's colour commentator. CFAC also brought in a young announcer from Toronto to act as the host for the 26 games the station would televise. A young Jim Van Horne, even then with his trademark dark thick moustache, joined CFAC after leaving CHUM to handle these duties. Meanwhile CBC's Hockey Night in Canada would chip in with six Saturday night telecasts of Flames home games, giving the team their only national exposure during the regular season.

The pre-season exhibition games did not give up much in the way of hints as to how the season would progress. Games were played at the Corral against the St. Louis Blues and Minnesota North Stars, who were being looked at as one of the top four Stanley Cup challengers for the upcoming season. The Flames also challenged the North Stars in an exhibition contest in Thunder Bay, Ontario. One thing for certain was 21 year old netminder Pat Riggin had earned a spot on the big club, making several stellar saves in the exhibition and would certainly complement if not challenge Dan Bouchard, the No. 1 goaltender. Calgary drew over 9000 fans to their exhibition games in the Corral and certainly looked like NHL hockey fever had struck the city.

The Flames left newly acquired defenseman Randy Holt, acquired in the Unger trade with the Kings, available in the waiver draft, but another club would not select him. Interestingly, Bobby Orr was available in the waiver draft although he had retired from the Chicago Blackhawks over a season before and Hartford left Bobby Hull unprotected although he had finally decided to retire. Calgary would make no selections from the players available in the waiver draft.

Chapter 6 – Opening Night

Thursday, October 9th, 1980 was the date hockey fans in Calgary had been waiting for, the first regular season National Hockey League game in the city. Once viewed as a pipe dream was now a reality. Calgary would battle the Quebec Nordiques in their first contest at the Corral. The Nordiques had gone through a transition the previous season as one of the anchors of the World Hockey Association that was allowed admittance to the NHL during the 1979 merger. Like the other WHA franchises to arrive in the NHL, the 1979-80 season was largely one to forget. The Nordiques finished third last in the league with 61 points, only the Winnipeg Jets and Colorado Rockies finished lower.

Going into the 1980-81 season looked to be equally disastrous for the Nords. Top scorer Rheal Cloutier was out with an injury for the start of the season and Marc Tardif was questionable after an injury during the pre-season. However, there was light at the end of this dark tunnel in the form of a group of brothers from the east side of the Iron Curtain. During the summer of 1980 Anton and Peter Stastny fled Communist dominated Czechoslovakia with the assistance of Nordiques management. The Stastny's were known to be gifted players on the international stage, but NHL prognosticators had no way of gauging Anton and Peter's efforts in Europe with the North American professional game.

With both teams facing the unknown, game one was sure to be memorable. The Corral was filled with a loud murmur as over 7000 fans looked for their seats and settled in for the evening. A red carpet affair was to take place for a ceremonial faceoff prior to the start of the game and the buzz in the building began to get louder as game referee Andy Van Hellemond jumped onto the ice. As Van Hellemond skated about Corral organist Irene Basse played "Light My Fire" by the Doors, never a more appropriate tune for the occasion.

After some words by Calgary mayor Ross Alger on the magnitude of the historic event, white Stetson cowboy hats were handed to Calgary resident Red Dutton, the first NHL president in league history; John Ziegler, the current NHL president; and Flames principal owner Nelson Skalbania. Following the rolling up of the carpet, the Corral crowd became louder as the Nordiques and Flames skated about in the warm-up then became quiet as Susie Smith got ready to sing the Canadian national anthem. At 7:52 pm Calgary's NHL history officially began as Van Hellemond dropped the puck between the Nord's Robbie Ftorek and Calgary's Guy Chouinard at center ice. Ftorek promptly drew the puck back to the Quebec zone and the game was on.

Although Ftorek won the opening faceoff Calgary came out like a house on fire! After Quebec sniper

Michel Goulet popped the first official NHL goal in Calgary behind Flames netminder Dan Bouchard at 8:10 of the first period. Calgary stormed back 35 seconds later, eventually getting two goals from Guy Chouinard and one from Willi Plett past Quebec goalie Michel Dion before the period ended. Dion was forced to hold his own in the first as Calgary outshot Quebec 17-6 during the opening period.

The second period looked no better as Kent Nilsson notched his first of the year at 4:55 of the second frame. Then Quebec came roaring back with the line of the Stastny brothers and first ever Atlanta Flames draft pick Jacques Richard doing much of the damage. Richard scored two goals during the period as Quebec scored three straight goals to even the score 4-4 at the end of the second. Quebec managed to do this while receiving two bench minors for too many men on the ice. These penalties were the result of the Stastny brothers leaving the bench too early during line changes, quite eager to take their turn on the ice.

During the third Calgary scored to take the lead with another Nilsson goal just over six minutes in, but Michel Goulet picked his second goal less than a minute later to tie. This game was a prime example of the wide open style of the NHL before the time goalies received larger and lighter equipment and defensive systems became the focus of all coaches during the regular season instead of just the playoffs.

Overtime was not played at this time in the NHL and the 7243 fans in attendance went home happy after Calgary tried several times to score late in the third. Ironically, Quebec seemed to be returning the favour to the Flames franchise as the Atlanta Flames played the Nordiques in their first NHL game at Le Collisee a year previous on October 9th, 1979! A 6-3 win for Atlanta.

Although a pile of rubber was thrown at both nets it was felt both Bouchard and Quebec's Dion had appeared shaky in net. Kent Nilsson could not believe what would be the tying goal, a short slap shot from along the goal line on the ice that was missed by Dion. However, opening night jitters in front of a boisterous crowd should be expected.

That first game gave Calgary fans a taste of what was to come. Hard fought contests every night as this mix of scorers and grinders never seemed to do things the easy way. The Flames were still located in the heavily competitive and much more eastern Patrick Division which had the 1980 Stanley Cup winners the New York Islanders and the runners up, the Pat Quinn coached Philadelphia Flyers. To top this off were the New York Rangers and the lowly Washington Capitals. But the Flames battled through it all going on to post the third best home record in the NHL and also set a franchise record for points with 92 during the 1980-81 season. Midway through the season general manager Cliff Fletcher shipped former No. 1

goaltender Dan Bouchard off to the very team they played in game number one, the Quebec Nordiques, for Jamie Hislop. This after deciding the team would be fine with the tandem of two young goalkeepers Pat Riggin and Reggie Lemelin. Fletcher also swung another deal obtaining the right winger Dan Labraaten from the Detroit Red Wings for Earl Ingarfield and Brad Smith.

While the Flames were largely successful there were problems. One was the team lacked a great deal of depth and this was most prevalent when the team lost members such as Ken Houston, Eric Vail and Don Lever to injuries and illness late in the season. Effectively three top forwards were missing and Calgary had little to call up to fill the holes. The other problem was the team really played its best at the Corral, but seemed to lose on the road.

Going into the stretch drive towards the playoffs the Flames had a string of seven games without a win going 0-5-2 prior to winning at home 5-3 over the down trodden Colorado Rockies, who had four regular players out of the lineup. And a 6-5 win over the Vancouver Canucks during the last game of the season.

Along with problems with depth and their road problems there was also cases where players were too aggressive or not aggressive enough. Coach Al MacNeil took Willi Plett aside instructing him on taking a bigger leadership role for the playoffs, but to also drop the many bad penalties he was drawing as their opponents continually capitalized on the power play. Plett publicly acknowledged in interviews that his play would need to improve for the playoffs. Offensively he had his best season with 38 goals but also set a career mark for penalties with 239 minutes. As Plett goes so do the Flames, in games won or tied he scored 31 of his 38 goals. Plett also pointed out his team needed to improve with more physical play in the last regular season games against Colorado and Vancouver in order to maintain home ice advantage and seventh place standing in the NHL. Ironically, the win over Colorado would be Calgary's first of the year having lost all three previous engagements. Defensively the team also needed to tighten up.

The Flames were also without a goaltender that had stepped up as the hot goalie in the stretch run. With Lemelin and Riggin more or less equally sharing the duties since Dan Bouchard was dispatched, neither had performed well enough to show the coaching staff "I am the number one man".

Calgary faced the possibility of playing one of these opponents in the first round of the 1981 playoffs; the Vancouver Canucks; Quebec Nordiques; or Chicago Blackhawks. The Canucks were the obvious choice as an opponent as they, like the Flames, played poorly down the stretch while the Nordiques had been on fire in a desperate race for a playoff spot. Chicago was the one choice Calgary hockey fans dreaded, as the Flames were 0-3 versus Chicago throughout the regular season.

The Flames 6-5 victory over the Canucks ensured their place with Chicago in the first round of the playoffs. Herald writer Jim Davies interviewed several fans for the April 6th column and reviews from season ticket holders on how the Flames would do ranged from getting by the first round to choking in the playoffs as in Atlanta. The team had not played very inspired hockey in the last weeks of the season. Davies also revealed that Oilers owner Peter Pocklington and Nelson Skalbania had friendly wagers going over the season with games involving the Oilers and Flames. Skalbania would be the winner as they went 2-1-1 over the Oilers.

Chapter 7 – The Playoffs Beckon

This was a whole new season and Calgary had a formidable opponent in the form of the Blackhawks. The Chicago club was the only one of 20 NHL opponents to not be defeated by the Flames during the regular season, quite a feat considering the balanced schedule the league then played under. The Flames had one loss and three ties versus the Hawks and each game was a closely fought battle with Chicago outscoring the Flames 12 to 11 in the four match ups. Not to mention, as an organization, the Flames had not won in Chicago Stadium in five seasons!

If there was one area the Blackhawks held an edge it was in goaltending as they had one of the best the NHL had ever seen in net. Even at age 37 Tony Esposito was still very much a part of the successes and failures of the Chicago franchise. Going into the 1981 first round matchup against the Flames Esposito's career records dwarfed those of Riggins and Lemelin. Esposito had over 5000 minutes of playoff experience versus only 20 minutes combined for the Calgary tandem of which all of those belonged to Rejean Lemelin and he played all of those in the 1979 playoffs versus Toronto during which he did not give up a goal. Esposito had been a member of the 1969 Montreal Stanley Cup winners as a bit member and had guided the Blackhawks to Cup final appearances in 1971 and 1973 losing in tough battles against the Canadiens. Neither Lemelin nor Riggin could compare against someone who manned the nets in the legendary 1972 Canada-Soviet hockey series.

   Tony Esposito would be the key to the series; at least that is what coach Al MacNeil thought. MacNeil felt that the Flames possibility of a win hedged on getting as many shots as possible on Esposito and continually having players drive to the net and create havoc. Shoot, shoot and shoot some more was the philosophy going into the series. As far as the young Calgary tandem went, MacNeil felt his goaltenders were the best combination currently in the league. He felt confident in either one starting, but delayed his selection for the net right up until game time.

   Wednesday, April 8th, 1981 would be the beginning of a test for this Flames club. Would they repeat the disastrous post-season runs of Atlanta or go on to new glory as Calgary Flames. What sort of team would show up, the club that at times dominated with physical play, potent offense and clutch goaltending or the squad that showed up inconsistently at the end of the season going 2-5-2 heading into the post-season.

   The Flames were equally as excited about this first ever playoff match up as the fans were. From team youngsters such as Brad Marsh to veteran Bob MacMillan, the Flames were nervous for game one of the series. The Blackhawks were somewhat nervous too, but a spirited practice at the Corral seemed to show nerves would not be a problem. The noise in the Corral was deafening as the Flames marched out of their dressing room and through the main lobby of the Corral. The Corral was a throwback to small town arenas most of the players had come through during their younger years. Walking through the lobby from the dressing room to the ice surface, past the throng of fans was just one of those things you did playing in Calgary.

One could cut the tension with a knife in the cozy confines, as nobody seemed to know what to expect, the fans, the officials and the players. The first playoff game in Calgary would be a test of nerves and strength. An announced crowd of 7226 watched and cheered for a different Flames team than the one that had performed poorly in the playoffs in Atlanta. The first period saw both teams circle each other like gladiators in a Roman Coliseum. The first period was a feeling out process as each team played a dump and chase game that was more out of an effort not to make a mistake as it was tightness in the minds of the Blackhawks and Flames players. Back and forth the play went and although there would be a number of good shots on goal Lemelin and Esposito were up to the task. As the seconds counted down on the score clock, Chicago and Calgary were caught in a scoreless draw by the first intermission. The Blackhawks were a tight checking team that made the most out of their opportunities to dig up loose pucks through hard work for scoring chances. The Flames could also play the Chicago style, as proved in the first frame, but they also could play it wide open too.

During the second period flashes of Calgary's offence came to life. Just over a minute into the first Bob MacMillan punched one past Esposito for a 1-0 Flames lead. The Flames kept coming with more scoring opportunities, Lever, Plett, Nilsson, Chouinard, MacMillan again and on and on. Calgary's forwards had only one area on the ice surface to drive for, the Chicago net. Lever broke in past the Chicago defence and only a prone Esposito using every inch of his body, stick and reach prevented Lever from making it 2-0. The former Vancouver captain could only watch helplessly as a great scoring chance disappeared in the form of a wobbling puck glancing off the goal post. Lever had been denied and No. 35 was keeping the Blackhawks in the game.

Line after line came swooping into the Chicago zone, each one adding to the Flames momentum. This was a team that neither Atlanta nor Calgary fans had seen before. They had seen snatches of this in other games, but not momentum building a drive that would continue to sustain itself. With Tony O' holding off the Flames charge, the thoughts of "here we go again" struck the Calgary faithful as a young rookie by the name of Darryl Sutter seemed to end the Flames explosion with his first ever post season goal, putting Chicago even with Calgary at 1-1 with about 2 minutes left in the second. Ironically, Sutter was an

Alberta boy from what was becoming a famous hockey family from the farm community of Viking northeast of Calgary. His brothers Brent and Duane played with New York Islanders and Brian played St. Louis. There were more hockey playing Sutters coming through the junior ranks, Ron and Rich who were the Lethbridge Broncos. Darryl's goal looked to be the shot that sent Calgary back to its Atlanta days.

Just before Calgary fans could get revved up again, Chicago struck again mere seconds later. Al Secord, now in his third season, put Chicago up 2-1 at 18:03 of the second period. It looked like the Atlanta curse had followed the team to Western Canada. Perhaps the ghost of General Sherman himself was torching the Flames playoff chances. But, these Flames did something the other Flames had not, the momentum prior to the two opposition goals was still there.

Defenseman Phil Russell banged in a goal to tie the score 2-2 just before the second ended. The Corral erupted perhaps a combination of surprise and jubilation. Had Russell's shot not eluded Esposito all the effort exerted by the Flames would have been for naught. Calgary continued the pressure into the third as Nilsson and Dan Labraaten scored for a 4-2 lead. Kent Nilsson had been in on every goal with a goal and three assists. Darryl Sutter once more scored to make it 4-3 but it was too late. Calgary had gone on to outshoot Chicago 26-15 in the last two periods and Riggin stood firm to give Calgary its first ever post season victory and the Flames franchise their first ever opening game victory in a playoff series.

The Flames had been a success in their opening act at the Corral. They had shown their speed, their skill and their grit. Midway through the third young Jim Peplinski tangled with Al Secord and Randy Holt took on Chicago's Terry Ruskowski moments later. The Flames showed they would not be intimidated, but would be the intimidators. It had been a game for the ages, possibly the most important game for the Flames franchise and the players responded.

However, one game does not make a series. A best of five does not allow for mistakes. One bad game could cause a shift in momentum and playoff success blown. With the best of five format an upset was always a great threat and Calgary, with a superior record, were the favourites although in the eyes of some Chicago was the favourite due to the Flames dubious playoff record from their Atlanta days.

The players had to jump back on the ice the very next night due to the way the NHL playoff format was structured. Again MacNeil instructed his team to continue pounding Tony Esposito with shots and hope that part of the onslaught of pucks squirts past. The Corral was on fire again that night, the crowd of 7226 roared with adoration as the Flames hit the ice. The crowd was a primarily male audience wearing suits, sport coats and collared shirts with very few of the team jerseys prevalent at games today. None of them certain if game one was an aberration or the look of things to come. Fortunately, the latter would be the case.

The Flames came out firing once again as they did during the first contest. The Flames forwards were once again buzzing the net, but Tony O' was once again up to the task. Esposito had been doing this for over a decade in Chicago and at times had largely the entire Blackhawks franchise riding on his shoulders. Not as vocal in the media as his more gregarious brother Phil, Tony Esposito was as much a competitor as his brother ever was.

A heavy slapshot from Bill Clement in the slot is gloved; Houston lets a wrist shot rip point blank and is denied. Guy Chouinard roars in amongst the Chicago defense and, caught out of his crease, once again Esposito goes diving back towards his net, stick, arms and body stretched enough to get his glove on the puck to deflect another scoring chance. Tony O' was a man who used every ounce of strength and courage to stop the enemy from scoring. All Chouinard could wonder, denied on this chance and other glorious opportunities in the first game, was if bad luck was to blame.

The shots continued to rain in on the Chicago net then a surprise, the red light behind Esposito lit up, Bob MacMillan had scored on a quick wrist shot from close in and the score was 1-0 Calgary midway through the first period. Each subsequent line picked up the momentum and Chicago looked overwhelmed by the speed of the Flames forward lines used in a quick European style transition game. It was becoming evident the Flames were the more skilled of the two clubs and Chicago could not put any pressure on either goalie Rejean Lemelin or the Flames defense. Calgary went to the dressing room with a 1-0 lead after outshooting Chicago 19-8 in the first frame. The score could have easily been 5-0 if not for Esposito's heroics.

One person witnessing Esposito's stellar play was a tall red headed young gentleman in the Flames executive box overlooking the ice surface at the Corral. Randy Gregg, a promising member of the Calgary based Canadian Olympic hockey team and also their team captain, was an invited guest of Flames management. The Flames were on the hunt for defensive talent and the 6'4" future doctor looked to be a good fit for the franchise. Gregg had just come off a year of playing in Japan and he would certainly be a nice addition to the Calgary line-up. The Edmonton Oilers had also courted Gregg and seeing he was on a medical internship at an Edmonton hospital, the Flames likely knew that the chance of signing him as a free agent was not great.

While conversations on a player's future went on in the Flames private box, the Flames and the

Blackhawks returned to the ice. One player on the Calgary roster who had yet to be heard from was the marvelously talented Kent Nilsson. Nilsson and his trademark Jofa "trash can" styled helmet had been shadowed throughout the first period by Rick Paterson who had not dressed for game one. Coach Keith Magnusson had benched defenseman Dave Hutchinson in favour of Paterson for this game with instructions to keep with Nilsson and not allow him any play making or goal scoring opportunities. This was to become the dawn of the era of "me and my shadow" with the most talented followed and harassed by the less talented. So far it had worked well when Magnusson could get his lines matched, but with Calgary having last change as soon as Paterson stepped on the ice, Nilsson would simply step off.

Magnusson eventually abandoned the scheme for the second period. The second seemed to imitate the first period, but Chicago seemed to have much more jump. Finally, Chicago got on the scoreboard as Al Secord scored his second goal of the playoffs from a feed from Tom Lysiak. Lysiak had been team captain for the Flames during the late 1970's before being traded to Chicago - a trade many said was just part of the eventual failure of the franchise in Atlanta. Lysiak was a talented two way player, well liked by his teammates and his curly locks were recognizable out on the ice to the fans. Good friend Willi Plett had openly stated Lysiak's departure was part of the cause of the Flames franchise downhill direction during the last days in Atlanta.

Calgary continued to respond to the challenge. More shots, more drives to the net sending bodies and ice chips spraying, but the Flames were beginning to fall on their heals as Chicago began doing more explorations within the Calgary defensive zone. However, most of the Chicago shots were coming from well out as the Flames defense was keeping the Blackhawks to the outside perimeter and Lemelin had very little in the way of the hard saves that Esposito had to make at the other end of the ice.

Bob MacMillan and linemate Guy Chouinard came roaring into the Chicago defensive zone set up by an outlet pass by defenseman Paul Reinhart. Chouinard feathered a pass over to MacMillan who tipped the black disk into the Chicago net to make the score 2-1 Calgary with less than four minutes left in the second.

Just as the announcements and cheering were subsiding after MacMillan's third goal of the game, the red light flipped on behind the Chicago net again. With players all around the goalmouth, Esposito had failed to stop Willi Plett's first marker of the playoffs. It was now 3-1 Calgary as the clock wound down, a somewhat comfortable lead heading into the second. However, two goal leads are hard for a team to defend. Teams tend to shut down offensively and go into a defensive shell with such a lead and it appeared this was happening to the Flames.

The other Marsh in the series, Chicago's Peter Marsh, scored early in the third to put the Hawks within one goal. But Calgary jumped back into the action with Kent Nilsson, sans pest Paterson, and Chouinard scoring with 85 seconds of Marsh's goal.

It looked to be over, a three goal lead for Calgary and Chicago appeared desperate and frustrated. Frustration was on the face of Al Secord as he and Randy Holt were involved in fisticuffs within moments of Chouinard's goal. Holt was becoming the Flames physical leader both with his fists and his body checks, this being his second altercation in two games. Both on the goal sheet and in the physical department, Calgary was winning the series. Bill Clement popped in another goal for the Flames making the final score 6-2. The Flames jumped on the ice congratulating Lemelin for his performance in net, a 40 save game with few of the quality shots Esposito had seen. Lemelin had proved himself quite capable in the Calgary net and for now he was the number one netminder. On the opposite end was Esposito who had earned some boos from some Calgary Flames fans for not coming out for the three star selection in both games at the Corral. However, this was the norm for the workmanlike goalie, always first on the ice and last off, adulation had little meaning - only victories counted.

While the Flames rejoiced they knew the biggest test was to come - battling Chicago and its boisterous fans inside the intimidating Chicago Stadium. As the franchise had not won in Chicago Stadium in five seasons, playing in the historic arena would be somewhat of a challenge.

Getting to Chicago turned out to be a challenge in itself, at least for the Blackhawks. Both the Blackhawks and Flames were scheduled to take the same flight from Calgary to Chicago to attend game three. However, NHL bylaws indicated that players from two separate franchises competing in a forthcoming game could not travel together. As a result Chicago general manager Bob Pulford needed to quickly make alternative arrangements in the form of a chartered flight.

One player looking forward to a possible game three victory was Flames defenseman Phil Russell. The helmetless Russell had originally played for the Blackhawks before being dealt to Atlanta during the 1978-79 season. Russell had been one of Chicago's top prospects and he still felt some resentment towards the organization for trading him. Russell had been one of the reasons Calgary had won the first two games of what the NHL officially called Series G. Reggie Lemelin had all sorts of help around the net. Calgary's defence was big and punishing, evinced by Brad Marsh during the second period of the last game. Marsh sent Chicago's Grant Mulvey,

Chicago's leading goal scorer from 1979-80, sprawling with a massive hit.

For all the talk of the Flames bumbling in the playoffs while in Atlanta, Chicago was equally inept during the same period. The late 1970s had not been kind to the Blackhawks and had not really posed a playoff threat since losing to the Montreal Canadiens in the 1973 Stanley Cup finals, that having been the season following Bobby Hull's departure to Winnipeg and the WHA. In fact the Blackhawks had a losing streak in the playoffs of sixteen straight playoff games until winning their first round match up against the St. Louis Blues during the 1980 playoffs.

The Blackhawks had a poor start to the 80-81 season. This was Keith Magnuson's first NHL head coaching job. Magnuson had just retired as an outstanding defenseman with the Blackhawks and was thrust into this new role. A passionate player over his 11 year career and well liked by both his Chicago teammates and his opponents, he literally drove his team into the ground during training camp and the first half of the regular season until Tony Esposito suggested he should relax his style as it was burning the team out during the grueling regular season. Then the Blackhawks began to play much better, even recording an eight game win streak as the team managed to go from missing the playoffs to tenth overall. Considering Chicago also faced a number of injuries to key performers such as Al

Secord, Grant Mulvey and Rich Preston, who was the second leading scorer on the club during 1979-80, the Blackhawks had performed well, all things considered.

Saturday, April 11th, 1981 would mark the Flames arrival into the Calgary era. The hallowed Chicago Stadium was tense. The usually raucous Chicago crowd seemed even more so that night. There were very few Flames fans in attendance other than those with a connection to the organization, which did not seem to matter to the Blackhawk faithful. Minority owner Norm Green was told by one Chicago fan what he could do with a small Flames pom-pom he had occasionally waved. The night previous the Chicago Bulls had played a National Basketball Association game against the Boston Celtics and the over zealous Chicago faithful sprayed a few Boston fans with beer. Fortunately, the Calgary fans did not receive the same reception.

One strange occurrence was the playing of only the Star Spangled Banner prior to the game and no O'Canada. Whether the arena staff thought the Flames were still located in Atlanta or Calgary was an American city was never told. Regardless, it was an oversight few in the crowd noticed along with the absence of a Canadian flag in the rafters for the game.

12482 witnessed one of the best games to date in the 1981 playoffs. Chicago proved it was ready early, trading goals with Calgary in the first period and constantly charging the Flames net. This time Reggie Lemelin had to provide Esposito like leadership in the nets making several stellar saves. At the end of the first it was a 2-2 tie and this wide open game had provided for 24 shots between the two teams. The Chicago crowd was quieted somewhat in the second as Bob MacMillan scored his fourth and Dan Lever his first of the playoffs to make it 4-2 Calgary going into the third period. It looked to be enough even though the Stadium's large pipe organ, believed to the largest in the United States, bellowed and the crowd began singing goodbye to coach Keith Magnuson. Then Chicago began mounting a comeback.

Al Secord scored his fourth of the series in a goal mouth scramble with only 2:48 left in the game. The crowd erupted and the Blackhawks kept up the pressure. Then Darryl Sutter struck with only 43 seconds remaining to tie the score 4-4, Sutter scoring from his belly on the ice after being up-ended by a Flames player. This would be the 48th shot Chicago would throw at the Flames net and Lemelin needed to be ready for more in overtime.

The Chicago Stadium was as loud as it had ever been. For as loud as the old rink could get and as boisterous as the crowds always were, they had only helped the Blackhawks win one NHL championship way back in 1961. Besides the crowd noise, the Flames had to contend with the warm humid conditions found in the Stadium that night. Everyone was drenched with sweat and drinking fluids was a top priority.

The first overtime period went by with both trying desperately for the win. The Blackhawks had the better of the period, dominating the first 15 minutes. Once again both goalies stood tall and amidst the hitting, slapshots and fast skating, the score still remained 4-4 after an extra 20 minutes.

With the clocks in the Stadium approaching one o'clock in the morning and well over four hours of hockey behind them, Willi Plett streaked across the blue line, the Flames having dominated play in the second overtime, and let what seemed to be a harmless shot head towards the net for what seemed destined for another routine Esposito save. This time the puck eluded Esposito's glove and the red light behind the Chicago net went on. The Flames jumped over the boards in jubilation at 15:17 of the fifth period. Plett had given the Flames their first ever franchise playoff series win. The tag of chokers could now be removed and Calgary was now a legitimate contender for the Stanley Cup.

Prior to the ending of that game, another momentous moment was being lived back in Alberta. At the Northlands Coliseum in Edmonton the Oilers had completed a three game upset over the Montreal Canadiens who had finished third overall in the league. While the Flames were doing battle with Chicago, many Canadians in Eastern Canada and northern Alberta were following Edmonton's playoff heroics on CBC. The Canadiens still have had many pieces remaining from their 1970s dynasty days and were picked by many to win back the Stanley Cup after a one year absence. With both Calgary and Edmonton's early playoff victories it would leave several days for speculation as to who their next opponents would be. Many even speculated immediately after their playoff wins that they might meet in the Stanley Cup finals! When the Flames arrived at Calgary International Airport the next afternoon over 500 cheering fans were waiting for them. This would be the first impromptu rally for Calgary's team, the first of many it was hoped!

Chapter 8 – Who is Next?

The players and fans waited to see who would be their second round opponent. Depending on how the other series ended up, the Flames could face one of the following; New York Rangers; Philadelphia Flyers; or the Minnesota North Stars. Due to their better regular season record the Flames would have home ice advantage against either the Stars or the Rangers, but not against the Flyers who finished five points better than Calgary in the standings. However, at this point, the Flames were as confident as ever, it is amazing what a playoff sweep can do!

The wait for the forthcoming second round on Thursday evening would give more time for Eric Vail, nicknamed "Train", to return from a groin injury that kept him out of the opening series. The Flames were a well conditioned club, as demonstrated in their domination of the second overtime period of game three.

As a result of their efforts the team practice on Monday, April 13th was a very loose affair. The Flames had earned a break for their overall outstanding efforts. However, at the Flames office at the Corral it was a different story. The phone was ringing off the hook with enthusiastic fans calling with words of support and encouragement for the franchise. It seemed all of Calgary was hockey mad, nothing like being a winner to drum up support. Even recently elected mayor Ralph Klein was excited about the turn of events, certain the Flames playoff dash would secure the future of the new arena proposed for the Winter Olympics and provide a greater focus on the drive for getting the 1988 games.

Meanwhile, the Flames remained idle waiting for the conclusion of the Philadelphia-Quebec and St. Louis-Pittsburgh series to see who they were up against in the second round. The Flyers had allowed the Nordiques to get back in the series, blowing a late two goal lead in game four of the best of five to force a fifth and deciding game. A Flyers victory meant home ice advantage for the Flames would be gone.

Ironically, the former Flames star goalie Dan Bouchard was the man between the pipes for Quebec - a teammate many of the former Atlanta players had a tough time understanding.

Coach Al MacNeil instructed his team to watch the Nordique-Flyer contest on TV as an exercise in scouting. With home ice on the line, the Flames were hoping Bouchard could pull off the upset. Unfortunately, Philadelphia bettered the best efforts of the Stastny brothers and their linemates. The Flyers would win 5-2 and this result combined with a St. Louis Blues victory made Calgary and Philadelphia the match up for the second round of the playoffs.

The Flames dutifully packed up their belongings and headed east for their Thursday night opening contest in Philadelphia. Calgary was ready for the Flyers, who each year looked less and less like the Broad Street Bullies that dominated the NHL during the mid-1970's. The always fierce Bobby Clarke was as intimidating as ever and Philadelphia was still a physically imposing team under the guidance of former Flyer teammate Pat Quinn. However, the Flyers were changing with the times. The league was becoming a more wide open league and players such as Ken Linseman, nicknamed "the Rat", and Brian Propp were forming the nucleus of the team's future. Aggressive and skilled players would be needed for the hockey of the 1980s and teams were beginning to see this trend with the Montreal Canadiens successes of the late 1970s. Quality statistics in the penalty killing and power play columns were more beneficial than those figures in the penalty minute column. Fighting and aggressive play with no direction would no longer work alone in determining the Stanley Cup winners.

Unfortunately, for the Flyers, the Broad Street Bully moniker still remained although the team that battled the New York Islanders in the 1980 finals was not nearly as potent as the clubs of five years before. In the 1981 playoffs the franchise had a defense composed primarily of minor league players from its affiliate in Maine. This was similar in many ways to the championship teams of 1974 and 75 which had largely a no name defense corps without the Bobby Orr and Brad Park like players of other clubs. The Flyers still reigned supreme over the league in penalty minutes, but this edition was not the real Broadstreet Bullies.

Philadelphia had two players on defense that were a minor concern to the Flames. Behn Wilson and Bob Dailey were both nursing injuries and were expected to have a limited role in the series. Dailey had been a surprise returnee for the Flyers as he had gone through a knee surgery only weeks before the start of the playoffs. Dailey was a force in the Quebec series, but then appeared limping in the corridors after the end of game five. Team physician Dr. Joe Tong would have to once again jump in to try and scuttle the injury bug in order to get Dailey back in the lineup.

The primary concern of the Flames management was the top Flyer line consisting of Ken Linseman, rugged Paul Holmgren, and talented scorer Brian Propp, who had been a stunning player for the Brandon Wheat Kings junior franchise. MacNeil assigned a line to cover the top line using tough man Randy Holt to get in the face of Holmgren and the others. It was generally felt that eliminating the production of the Linseman line would make the task of scoring fall on the hands of the Flyers lesser forwards and stay at home defense.

With that it seemed Calgary had all the answers for a series with the Flyers. Philadelphia had also played a more grueling first round than Calgary and the Flames were fortunate in only losing role players Dan Laabraten and David Hindmarch to minor groin and knee injuries respectively.

Calgary's speed at forward and rushing defenseman Paul Reinhart should give the Flyers rookie defense something to think about every shift. With Philadelphia having played a brutal seven games over thirteen days Philly certainly must have been tired and Calgary was ready to take advantage of it. The Flames were confident and there were suggestions they would sweep the first two games of the series at the Spectrum in Philadelphia coming home to Calgary with a 2-0 advantage.

On Thursday, April 16th, 1981 the answers to these predictions would begin to emerge. Game One would leave the Flames looking for answers themselves. MacNeil countered the Rat Patrol, the nickname for the Linseman line, with some poison control of his own in the form of Jim Peplinski, Willi Plett and Randy Holt. However, their success in game one was less than great. Just over three minutes in Paul Holmgren scored to make it 1-0 Flyers. Then the Flyers struck again when under-rated winger Bill Barber scored his sixth goal of the playoffs. Calgary headed to the dressing room down 2-0 and were both badly outshot and outplayed. It looked as though the layoff had hurt the Flames and the supposedly tired Flyers seemed to have not missed a beat. With two more goals in the second, including another from Holmgren, it was 4-0 going into the third. A late flurry of Flames scoring chances were denied by Flyer goalie Rick St. Croix as he went on to a 35 shot shutout victory in front of 17077 roaring Flyers fans. The Philly defense did their job and the Rat Patrol did theirs. However, a foretelling of what was to come was evident in the Calgary's morning practice. Both coach MacNeil and assistant Pierre Page were hit in the face by pucks deflected off the sticks of Kevin Levallee and Pat Riggin respectively and would not be behind the bench for game one. Philadelphia had early control of the best of seven series one game to none.

This turn of events forced Al MacNeil to look at changing goaltenders for the next night's game. Reggie Lemelin had played tremendously well in the Chicago series and did a fine job in game one, but things needed to be shaken up. Pat Riggin would get the call for game two. While the assigning of Riggin to the Calgary net was not a surprise the move Pat Quinn made was.

Quinn decided to rest game one starting goalie Rick St. Croix and insert Pete Peters. Quinn told the media he felt it would be better to spell St. Croix off as the Flyers will have played nine games in thirteen nights coming into game four of the series. Quinn worried

St. Croix might be too tired and felt if he was going to make a move he should do so now.

Calgary was now looking for one win before returning home. With thoughts of a two game sweep at the Spectrum dashed, the Flames wanted a split so they would get home ice advantage from the Flyers. Besides a 2-0 hole would not be an easy one to climb out of. However, as young singer Andrea McArdle stepped out onto the Spectrum ice surface to sing the national anthems, a part of Flames history from Atlanta still remained. The franchise had not won at the Spectrum since October 22nd, 1978 and this remained as one of the last demons to be exorcised. Would game two see the end of that streak and a needed split for the Flames?

In fact Flyers fan Dave Leonardi had it summed up in print for all to see as game one came to a close. Leonardi was known as "the signman" by the faithful at the Spectrum. Every game he brought a number of home made signs with messages of encouragement for the Flyers and observations of their opponents. A Hockey Night in Canada camera focused in on this particular sign's message stating the sad fact - "Same Old Flames".

As the roar after the Star Spangled Banner quieted down, the Philly colours of bright orange with black began to intertwine with the Flames red. This kaleidoscope of colour would swirl around the

Spectrum ice in front of another sold out crowd of over 17000 for the next 60 minutes. It soon became clear that Calgary would need a strong performance between the pipes in order to not be demolished by the Flyers.

Riggin had not played over the last two weeks, forced to watch his counterpart Reggie Lemelin in the first series and the last match up in this series. Philadelphia seemed ready for this game, even more so than Game One's drubbing. They began pelting Riggin with shots early in the first period as they did in the first game. The Flyers also repeated their earlier success by jumping out to a 1-0 lead just over five minutes in. Bill Barber notched his seventh goal of the post-season with Behn Wilson and Rick MacLeish grabbing assists.

With several opportunities to make it 2-0 dashed by Riggin, Paul Reinhart tied the game with his first goal of the playoffs at 12:34 of the first frame. Philadelphia and Calgary traded goals again, by the end of the first it was 2-2 although the Flyers had the edge in play. But, the first period had not been without some controversy. The Flames bench erupted when Mel Bridgeman collapsed on the ice just outside the Philadelphia defensive zone. Referee Ron Hoggarth immediately raised his hand to signal a penalty and a slashing call. Willi Plett was given a five minute major for the infraction. Bridgeman simply skated away after Plett left the ice, obviously not in much pain.

The second period was all Calgary from a scoring perspective and Riggin continued to be a stalwart in net. Houston, Plett and recent arrival Jaime Hislop made it 5-2 for Calgary going into the third period. However, the Flyers were not going to give up.

Philadelphia turned the heat on and limited Calgary to two shots in the third period while throwing nineteen at the Flames net. Coach Pat Quinn even shifted the leading scorer on the team, Bill Barber, from his left wing position into the regular defensive rotation midway through the third for some extra offensive punch. Just past the thirteen minute mark Behn Wilson found the back of the net to make it 5-3. Then Tom Gorence struck at 17:08 to make the score 5-4.

The Flyers looked to be well on their way to a tie game as they continued getting shots on Riggin. One thing for certain the Flyers had pride, there was never a team in the NHL more competitive in a closely fought contest. Quinn pulled Pete Peters in order to get an extra attacker, but the Flames withstood the charge. With seconds to go Willi Plett justly found the puck on his stick and dumped it down into the Flyers end of the rink. The Flames could finally celebrate, they had escaped the Spectrum with a 5-4 win and the series was tied 1-1.

Calgary fans were ecstatic and they also had a new hero. Pat Riggin had been exemplary in goal during his 42 save performance. Without his heroics the Flyers would have easily been winners and up 2-0 in the series. The victory had broken a Spectrum curse for the Flames that dated back to 1978.

After the game Riggin seemed quite laid back about his performance, his only concern seeming to be the return flight home to Calgary. While he could handle the Flyers, Riggin could not handle flying. However, he would forget his flying concerns upon arrival at Calgary International as over 200 fans greeted the team with cheers, just as they did after their triumphant return from Chicago. "Flames Fever" had certainly captured the city and the players were quite appreciative of it, especially those who endured the Atlanta days.

One player who would miss out on the reception would be forward Bert Wilson. Wilson suffered an eye injury from an errant stick during the first game at the Spectrum and would be forced to stay in Philadelphia as the rest of his teammates jetted home to Cowtown. Due to the nature of the injury there was some worry that the change of air pressure experienced during air travel could cause damage. Fortunately, the injury was not considered serious although Flames team doctor Nick Kastalen accompanied Wilson to hospital.

Calgary fans were looking forward to Sunday night's Game Three at the Corral. The Corral, the arena that was much maligned for its quaint size and devoid of the attributes the NHL was looking for, was suddenly being looked at in the same way the Boston Garden or the Montreal Forum was looked at, a harsh environment for the opposition to win. During the regular season the Flames lost only five games out of their forty home dates, quite an accomplishment for a team that had come from a city where home ice advantage meant very little. Flames fans were hoping the Corral's undefeated post-season streak would continue.

The Corral was rocking that evening. Many observers felt the crowd was the loudest it had ever been. The facility that was an adequate fill in for the team was now playing host to a quarter-final match up. Few during the regular season would have believed it.

Pat Quinn decided to go back to St. Croix for the third game, MacNeil, obviously, sent Riggin back to the net. While Lemelin had done wonders against Chicago and did not embarrass himself against in the face of a constant Flyer attack, Riggin was now the hot goalie and had earned his spot with game two's performance.

Amidst the din in the Corral was Nelson Skalbania. Skalbania had yet to see his Flames play in the NHL

Stanley Cup tournament. Family matters and business dealings in Vancouver had kept him away. Initial worries from some fans and city officials about problems with absentee ownership were dashed when the Flames took to the ice for their first game. By then most people were only concerned with the product in the arena and not the politics of business. Unbeknown to the Calgary fans in attendance that night, Skalbania was not only in town to see his team play, but also to complete another business transaction. The *Calgary Herald* reported the next day that Skalbania was negotiating a further sale of his interest in the team to the other shareholders in the franchise.

On the ice the Flyers seemed to have not missed a beat from the end of game two at the Spectrum. This time the Flames caught some luck in the form of two early penalties sending Reid Bailey and Behn Wilson to the penalty box very early in the first. Calgary would have a short 41 second long two man advantage with both Flyer defensemen in the sin bin. Kent Nilsson looked clear to score on a cross-ice feed from the offensively gifted Paul Reinhart.

Unfortunately, Nilsson's shot towards a virtually empty net with St. Croix out of the play sailed a good stick length wide. Nilsson looked somewhat frustrated, as did the energetic Flames fans. In a tight game against their opponent Calgary had to cash such gifts in. The hot power play that had been a great help in the Chicago series was suddenly growing cold.

Frustration gave way to jubilation as Don Lever accepted a nice pass into the center ice area from Guy Chouinard then fired it past St. Croix into the Philadelphia net. The Corral sounded like it was going to fall apart at the seams! At 5:25 of the first period Calgary had a 1-0 lead, the first early Flames lead of the series. However, the enthusiasm over the early lead would be tempered by the constant buzzing of the Flames net by the Flyers.

The game being played on the Corral ice surface was the full throttle hockey the 80s would be noted for. However, the game remained close in large part to both goaltenders and defensemen exceptionally skilled at getting rid of loose pucks and tying up enemy forwards around the net.

Within 20 seconds of each other, Brad Marsh and Bob Murdoch were sent to the penalty box. Philadelphia would have a chance at a two man advantage. At 9:54 of the first frame, the Flyers Rick MacLeish wasted no time in tying the game. MacLeish let go a blazing shot at Riggin. Riggin had made the save but the puck flipped end over end off his goalie pad and over his body and into the net. Only fifteen seconds after getting their two man advantage Philadelphia had capitalized. This would be the first dint in the Calgary goalie's armour and the

Flyers hoped for more.

For as good a transition game the Flames had, the Calgary players noted that the Flyers were equally adept. Philadelphia's no name defense always seemed more than capable to get the puck to a forward turning to head out of the defensive zone. Quick passes were the name of the game for both teams. Philly's defense that was expected to be the most vulnerable part of their team seemed to be their strength.

After the first period it was 1-1 and the second period would not be a good one for the Flames. The team squandered two power play opportunities during the second period, one coming with the first minutes of the drop of the puck. Pat Riggin only became busier. Although the Flyers would not score, "Rigs", as he was known to his teammates, kicked, gloved and deflected nineteen shots during the period. Calgary only could come up with seven on St. Croix at the other end of the ice. It may have been during this period that many realized Pat Riggin was for real and his game two performance was not a fluke.

Riggin flopped about making save after save. He wielded his Wally brand goalie stick and right handed catching glove as though they were simple extensions to his body. Several times he denied glorious chances, many of those in the form of odd man rushes towards the Flames net. The Calgary defensive zone seemed to be filled with two on three or two on one situations. As much a product of enthusiastic Flames racing up ice to convert a rush into a goal as it was defensive lapses, Riggin was there to bail his mates out. At the end of the second it was still tied and the Flames were badly out shot and out chanced.

While the Flames, with the exception of Don Lever, had trouble scoring and generating offense, there was another person capable of scoring in the arena that night. This young figure stepped out of the Corral crowd and onto the ice. Gripping the stick handed to him very tightly; Alan Kent had the opportunity of a lifetime. Kent was attempting to put the puck through a small opening cut into a piece of plywood stretched out across the net. Sponsored by Cowley and Keith, the second intermission shoot to win contest was a staple of Corral home games and many other rinks across North America during games. Kent shot the puck down the ice and through a small hole which was only slightly larger than the rubber disk itself. Kent's prize for his efforts was $1000, not a sum of money to sneeze at.

As the third period began and progressed into the evening the Philadelphia Flyers must have wondered whether the arena staff had forgotten to take the board out of the net after intermission! Riggin continued to keep the Flames in the game.

Then the Calgary faithful, on the edge of their seats

with "oohs" and "aahs", began to cheer widely. Rugged Willi Plett had done it again. His fifth goal of the playoffs put Calgary up 2-1 with just over seventeen minutes left in regulation time.

As usual, Philadelphia would not give in and those final seventeen minutes were nail biters for many at the Corral that night. Calgary failed to capitalize on a power play for the seventh time that evening, this time with Ken Linseman in the box. This was going to be a great concern to Al MacNeil as the Flames success on the powerplay had been part of the reason the Chicago series had gone so well.

As the minutes ticked down it looked more and more as though the game would depend on the goaltender wearing number one for the Calgary franchise. With well under a minute remaining the slippery "Rat" found the puck on his stick. With each stride Ken Linseman was closer to the Calgary net and overtime. Legs pumping, the bright orange Flyers jersey got closer to the Calgary net. Fans around the Corral were slowly beginning to rise in anticipation of what might or might not happen. A lone figure stood between Linseman and glory, clad in white with dashes of red and yellow trim, and a large flaming C on his chest. The red Cooper helmet of Pat Riggin moved with the flow of the orange and black clad figure approaching, the dark eyes within moving with the motions of the opponent. The Flyers offensive threat tried a quick move to pull Riggin out of position. The large goal stick taped with black stick tape lunged out from the uniform of white and red. Pat Riggin caught just enough of the Rat's stick to thwart another Philadelphia opportunity. The Corral once again roared in approval as the puck drifted away from the Flames net, the last attempt the Flyers had. Calgary had done it; they had won 2-1 and were up two wins to one in the series.

With much attention focused on Andy Moog's outstanding postseason performance for the Edmonton Oilers making headlines, Pat Riggin was going to give him company following game three. Riggin was without a doubt the number one star during the three star selections after the game. There were comparisons to Ken Dryden's 1971 performance that helped Montreal to the Stanley Cup. Many began believing this would be the year Calgary would put its name on that coveted trophy. Riggin had made 47 saves on 48 shots, an amazing performance for any goaltender and superb for a second year goalie in only his second career playoff game. With two tough victories and a plethora of outstanding saves behind him, Riggin was the toast of Calgary. Unfortunately, he would only have to do it again the next day; there was no time to bask in the glow of his game three performance.

Game four would give Calgary players and fans thoughts of something they had thought about, but had not really come to believe. They quite possibly could be the next Stanley Cup champions. The fourth game of a series is a pivotal contest in the evolution of a best of seven playoff series. Win the game and your team is up three games to one with another three chances to win. Lose the game and it is left to a best of three where anything could happen.

The Flames wanted this game badly. With the absence of Pat Riggin's heroics, the Calgary squad could be down 3-0 in the series. The Flyers desperately needed this game as only two teams in National Hockey League history had ever come back from a 3-1 deficit to win a series. The Rat Poison line of Peplinski, Holt and Willi Plett had been very effective against the Flyers number one line lead by Ken Linseman. The only scoring Linseman, Holmgren and Propp had accomplished was on power play opportunities or when MacNeil could not get his checking line out against them. However, Pat Quinn kept sending his top line out with the exterminators right behind them. Calgary had been effective in shutting the top line down, but this did not concern Quinn.

The Flyers and Flames threw themselves into game four. Again the key match up seemed to be the checking Plett line against the scoring Linseman line. These six men; Peplinski; Holt; Plett; Linseman; Holmgren; and Brian Propp had done battle for days. Monday, April 20th, 1981 would be no different and frustrations would set in.

Calgary seemed to have the jump they needed in this pivotal game early. Ken Linseman was penalized early, giving another opportunity for the anemic Calgary power play. However, Calgary could not convert. Jamie Hislop and Bill Clement, who had been excellent in killing numerous power play opportunities for the Flyers, came up with a goal early in the first. Then there was another opportunity with Hislop banging the puck in past Rick St. Croix during an even strength situation. Frustration was getting to the Rat Patrol as Ken Linseman took another penalty midway through the first, negating a power play for his mates with Bob Murdoch sitting in the penaly box designated for the Flames. On a powerplay opportunity late in the period the Linseman line would knock in a goal to tie the game 1-1. Paul Holmgren would get his fifth goal of the playoffs. As the clock ran down to zero, Calgary, for the first time in the series, had gained some control over their pesky Philly opponents.

Play during the second was even, but Calgary pulled ahead. Peplinski notched his first career postseason goal at 6:38 and Don Lever grabbed his third of the playoffs 32 seconds later. It would be a 3-1 Calgary lead heading into the third. Both teams had quieted down from the solid hitting and penalty filled first period. Calgary looked to be on their way to a 3-1 series lead. However, as they had in the previous matches, the Flyers gave it their all in the third.

Referee Bob Myers would be busy in the third trying to keep the Linseman and Plett lines under control as their style of play grew more ferocious, each shift against each other looking similar to the last one. As Linseman, Holmgren and Propp began stepping over the boards the Calgary bench would stir. Peplinski, Holt and Plett would then step over the boards and onto the ice. Then a ballet consisting of boarding, elbows and taunting would begin. Peplinski battling with Linseman; Holt chasing after Holmgren; Willi Plett and Brian Propp verbally sparring with each other. When they were not taunting each other they were arguing with the referees and linesmen. Three games of this were finally wearing thin, but had yet to erupt into a significant encounter.

While the Linseman and Peplinski units did battle with each other the Flyers continued to press and they were rewarded not once, but twice before the third period was ten minutes old. Rick MacLeish and Bobby Clarke had scored to tie the game at 3-3. The Flames seemed to have let another lead slip away in the late going. The once raucous Corral crowd was now growing somewhat quieter and more tense. After two periods where the Flames seemed to dictate the play, a first in the series, if this had been a boxing match the Flyers may have already won by technical knockout. However, character is often defined in sports as being able to come back from adversity. A tie game with just over ten minutes to go does not get much more adverse.

Then right at the ten minute mark of the third something happened at the Corral that had never happened before. Randy Holt, the scrappy seven year NHL veteran and Paul Holmgren's feisty shadow, scored his first goal of not only the playoffs, but the entire season. The Corral crowd was apoplectic and feeling much better about the home team's chances. Once again Calgary had matched a Philly scoring outburst, it was now 4-3 for the Flames.

Checkers were now scorers, as Holt repeated his efforts with another goal converting a feed from Jim Peplinski as he did with his first goal. The Flames bench and the rest of the arena went wild. Suddenly Randy Holt was the second coming of Bobby Hull. He looked as surprised as he was enthusiastic just over four minutes after scoring his first goal. However, the Flyers, as usual, would not surrender.

With the Peplinski line still matched up with the Linseman line, all hell broke loose just two ticks past the fifteen minute mark of the third. After another Flyer scoring chance a large scrum formed to the left of Pat Riggin's net. Peplinski, Holt, Linseman, Propp, Plett and Holmgren began pushing and shoving with Flames defensemen Phil Russell and Brad Marsh thrown in for good measure. The taunting, sweater pulling and pushing resulted in game misconduct penalties to all the forwards on the ice on both clubs except one. Paul Holmgren escaped without a penalty from referee Bob Myers to the amazement of the Corral crowd and the Calgary bench. As a result of all the penalties a three on three situation developed on the ice. This was a hallmark of the then wide-open NHL.

With only six skaters out on the ice surface, there would be all sorts of opportunities for creative play. With the score 5-3 for Calgary Bill Barber, Bobby Clarke and Behn Wilson took the next shift for this situation. Promptly Clarke put the puck over to Barber and it was now 5-4. The Corral crowd once again would have to witness another stunning finish. Mel Bridgeman, who had drawn a controversial call earlier in the series, managed to put a startle into the crowd by blasting the puck past Riggin and off the goal post late in the game. However, it would be too late. Calgary won and the Flames were one win away from the Stanley Cup semi-finals, something many observers would never have dreamed possible at the start of the year. The Corral and the adoring Calgary fans were undefeated in the 1981 playoffs.

Thoughts were now going to the game five rematch in Philadelphia at the Spectrum. This was after all the hometown of the fictional hero Rocky who had become a part of the city's folklore as though he had been a mythological character from an ancient civilization. The Spectrum was an intimidating place to play during routine regular season contests, one could imagine it will only be worse for a deciding game.

It was this belief that one Philadelphia newspaper scribe decided to remain in Calgary for the return engagement, game six. Jay Greenberg was counting on the Flames folding under the pressure of the Spectrum crowd and the Flyers backed into a corner. Just like a wild animal with nowhere to go, the Flyers would fight to the death to win as they had in every other deciding game since they began their Stanley Cup runs in the mid-1970s. Down three games to one in the best of seven series, Greenberg had seen this team react to such situations before and knew Calgary might be feeling a tad over confident. In hockey such over confidence can be trouble to the team that exudes it.

Calgary was still a very loose and confident bunch going into game five. Unfortunately, Kent Nilsson would be forced to remain in Calgary as he had suffered a bad charley horse during game four and was continuing to undergo therapy with the hopes he would be ready for the next series or in the worst case scenario, a game six. However, the Flyers also had key injuries including Paul Holmgren. Holmgren had injured his hand and defenseman Bob Dailey was still out with an aggravation of a previous knee injury. Bert Wilson must have seemed like the forgotten Flame. He still remained in Philadelphia at the Wills Eye Hospital. There was hope Wilson's left eye was still improving. Although unlucky getting the injury, the facility he was in was one of the best at the time for treating eye injuries. As he settled in to listen to the radio broadcast of game five, all he needed to do was listen to the play by play of the first period.

As expected the Spectrum was loud and the Flyers played like their life depended on it. Pat Quinn, who had told reporters the shadow line Calgary was using on the Linseman line was having no effect, decided to change strategy. At every possible opportunity the Linseman line came off when the Plett, Peplinski, Holt combination went out. The result was three goals for Brian Propp and three assists for Ken Linseman during the first period. By the end of the first period it was 4-1 Philadelphia, the Flyers heavily out chancing and out hitting Calgary and the shot clock showing 13 for the home squad and only three for the visitors. An early score by Ken Houston in the second gave the Flames a wee bit of hope, but two more Flyers goals effectively finished the game for the Flames. However, it had been clear from the first ten minutes of the contest it was over. There was really nothing Pat Riggin could do. He had been overwhelmingly responsible for the three Flames victories thus far, but the magic was not there this night. Philadelphia had won 9-4 and Calgary fans that had taken the win streak in stride at the Corral were quite confident a game six Flames win was only a matter of dropping the puck. Some were already looking towards the possible semi-final opponent

Calgary would face. The media had already picked up on the fact a New York Rangers victory against the defending champion Islanders would guarantee home ice advantage for the Flames in the Stanley Cup final!

However, there was one big blonde haired problem for the Flames. One of their key leaders, Willi Plett, would be forced to watch the game and not participate in game six. During the lopsided 9-4 loss Plett was given a pair of game misconduct penalties. Plett received his first such penalty from referee Ron Wicks for jumping Flyer Glen Cochrane after he had taken a poke at Jim Peplinski from behind during a melee midway through the second period. After the ensuing scrum Plett then tried getting at Mel Bridgeman who was on his way to the Flyer dressing room down the same corridor Plett was taken to the visitor's locker room. That gave Wicks incentive to place a second misconduct on Plett. As a result the double misconduct called for an automatic game suspension. Plett would have to serve his suspension immediately. The Flames appealed the suspension to no avail. Al MacNeil and Cliff Fletcher both insisted the misconduct calls were unjust and that Bridgeman goaded Plett into action after a verbal taunt. Fletcher even went on to insist that this had been the Flyers style of play since their entry into the league in 1967. Unfortunately, the Plett appeal was denied and game six would go on without him.

Another player left looking in was Pat Riggin.

MacNeil decided to put Reggie Lemelin back in after the terrible 9-4 loss at the Spectrum. Lemelin was well rested and ready. The flight back to Calgary had been very quiet with most of the Flames grabbing some extra sleep after their ordeal in Philadelphia. However, the Corral and its undefeated streak were ahead. Everyone hoped it would continue and thoughts of a game seven battle for it all at the Spectrum were somewhat unsettling.

   The Corral was once again home sweet home for the Flames, but the home club looked somewhat tentative for game six. Although they were in the Flyers end frequently the hometown team could not get a lead on which they could build on. Neither could Philadelphia and into the second period the game was scoreless. Don Lever missed a glorious chance to score on the empty side of the net being one of the more memorable opportunities missed for Calgary.

   Then the same line that had done all the damage in game five did it again. Ken Linseman notched his third goal of the series off a Holmgren assist making it 1-0 for the Flyers. Holmgren had managed to chase down Paul Reinhart and hook him in order to get the puck and send it out from the boards to Linseman. Calgary fans were incensed referee Andy Van Hellemond had missed this call and voiced their displeasure, as did the Flames bench. Van Hellemond also did not make a call on Glen Cochrane for mugging Bob Murdoch along the boards prior to the

Linseman goal.

Less than twenty seconds after the Linseman goal and Calgary fans still discussing the uncalled penalties, the man who had personified the Flyers for well over a decade struck and it was 2-0 Philadelphia. Bobby Clarke had his third postseason marker. Game six was looking to be a repeat of the drubbing at the Spectrum. Then the Corral was brought back to life when Guy Chouinard scored on Rick St. Croix from center ice on a long shot that should have been an easy save late in the period.

Now 2-1 it looked to be another rip-roaring finish when Brian Propp stole the puck from Brad Marsh just outside the Calgary blue line, roared in towards the Calgary net with Ken Linseman. Propp then fed Linseman a perfect pass as Calgary defenseman Phil Russell tried to break up the two on one opportunity. All Linseman had to do was fire the puck at the net and the third goal to elude Reggie Lemelin had been completed. Linseman and company had struck again. Another hectic third period would follow, but it was all but over with the second Linseman marker. A 3-1 Flyer win and back to the city of brotherly love for game seven.

However, the Flames faithful were mad as hell at Van Hellemond for the calls he missed leading to Philadelphia's first goal and other calls that were questionable in the eyes of the Calgary fans. Some of the Corral's occupants threw trash on the ice at the end of the game, others threw debris at Van Hellemond and his two linesmen as they left the ice. This prompted a somewhat overreaction as the Calgary City Police were called upon to escort the NHL officiating crew back to their hotel in the event some disgruntled fan wanted to discuss matters further. The only problem after the game was Randy Holt getting a gross misconduct penalty for telling Van Hellemond that his non-calls cost the Flames the game. Willi Plett's aggressive play was certainly missed, fortunately he would be ready to appear at the Spectrum.

   The looseness of the Flames after the game four victory was gone, replaced with caution and some concern. A series clinching game seven in Philadelphia was not the script the Flames had been reading, but here it was. This would be the biggest test of the Flames franchise since its inception. The rowdy crowds that filled the Spectrum in game one, two and five would even be more of a factor in a game seven.

   The Calgary Flames had also become the darlings of the Canadian media now that the Edmonton Oilers went down to defeat at the hands of the defending champion New York Islanders. Even American sports publication Sports Illustrated was scrambling for material on the Flames. CBC's entire national network would be broadcasting this pivotal game, as

Calgary was the last Canadian franchise standing in the playoffs. That alone was attracting a great deal of fans.

The Spectrum was filled with bedlam for game seven and would truly be rocking that night. The Flyers might have had an unfair advantage in that they had a couple of good luck charms. The national anthem singer Andrea McArdle had never sung prior to a game the Flyers had lost. The other was in the form of Chuck Barris. Yes, the same Chuck Barris who was host of the Gong Show, a well-known 1970s television game show. Barris had never attended a Philadelphia Flyers contest in which the Flyers were the losers. Flyers owner Ed Snider even cajoled Barris into coming with the team to Calgary for game six. As a result the Flyers were victors in five of the five games Barris had attended. He and Flyers management were hoping to make that six for six on this night.

While the hometown club had some lucky charms the Flames were becoming philosophers. Brad Marsh thought that the series had been fairly even and Calgary was due to win after two consecutive losses. The Flames were ready for the greatest test of their playoff drive.

Would Calgary be able to withstand the ferocious Flyers and their vocal fan support? What Calgary team would show up, the ineffective club from the game five blowout or the scrappy grinders from game four? Would Pat Riggin, MacNeil's game seven selection for the net, put on another stellar performance as he had earlier in the series? So many questions and only one answer, game seven.

The Flyers managed to get into penalty trouble early and Calgary capitalized. With Brian Propp in the penalty box for a bench minor it would be a familiar face of a returnee to the Flames lineup taking advantage. Willi Plett scored his sixth playoff goal on a Guy Chouinard pass at 3:03 of the first period. The Flames got what they wanted with an early lead in this pivotal game. The Spectrum suddenly grew a little quieter.

Calgary was keying in on the recent additions to the Flyers lineup, their replacement defense. They did this by keeping close to the Flyer forwards and cutting off the opportunity for a quick outlet pass. More often than not the Flyers defense were being forced to ice the puck or risk losing it on a give-away in their own end or the neutral zone. It was working very well for Calgary.

Then Paul Holmgren was given a penalty and once again Calgary's power play went to work. This would be the second of the three penalties Holmgren would draw during the period. Unlike the others this one cost Philadelphia. Ken Houston scored his fifth off another Chouinard pass and it was 2-0 Calgary at

8:33 of the first. Calgary kept the pressure on the Flyers forwards and defense thus effectively neutralizing the hometown crowd. The Flames had also stopped the Flyers effective dump and chase routine they had been so successful with in their victories that had pressured Calgary's defense into making mistakes. As in game five the game appeared to be over, this time in the Flames favour, by the end of the first period.

Rookie Kevin Lavalle would score for Calgary in the second and Flyer veteran Bill Barber would answer to give the Flyers a small ray of hope. With the score 3-1, Bob MacMillan would make it 4-1 Calgary with a goal of his own. There would be no comeback this time and the Flyer faithful knew it. With over five minutes remaining in the third period at least one third of the Spectrum crowd had gone home. As the clock clicked down Brad Marsh hugged a jubilant Pat Riggin and the rest of the Calgary team poured on to the Spectrum ice, excitedly joining in the celebration. It was over after seven gruelling games, Calgary had bested the Philadelphia Flyers and they were now on their first trip to the Stanley Cup semi-finals in team history.

After the game, with the Spectrum seats sitting in empty silence, *Calgary Herald* reporter Jim Davies witnessed a lone figure stepping out on to the ice surface. This tall distinguished blonde haired figure looked around his surroundings. Tossing a puck in his hands, he continued to look about, deciding finally it was time to go. The figure then hurled the rubber disk at the Plexiglas surrounding the Spectrum ice surface, the puck making a distinctive "CLINCK" sound and then rebounding onto the ice, sliding harmlessly along. The figure then took one last look as he stepped off the ice. Willi Plett finally believed it, they had beat Flyers and they would not have to return to Philadelphia until next season. According to the reporter who witnessed this, all Plett could do was smile.

The Flames organization had chartered an aircraft from Pacific Western Airlines to bring Calgary's conquering heroes home. Many observers thought Calgary would fold in the seventh game, instead it was the Flyers who looked tired and beaten. The sad sack Flames were now in the final four. Upon arrival at Calgary International the Flames faithful were once again waiting to greet them. Calgary was once again celebrating as a city, ahead loomed the Minnesota North Stars.

Chapter 9 – The Cup is Close at Hand

While Calgary was rejoicing in the exploits of their NHL heroes, the Flames were not the only hockey game in town this late in the season. Calgary's Western Canadian Junior Hockey League entry, the Wranglers, was one victory away from reaching the Memorial Cup tournament to be held in Windsor, Ontario. The Calgary Wranglers had a stranglehold on the Western Hockey League championship final leading the Victoria Cougars three wins to one in the best of seven series.

The Wranglers were performing their magical run through the playoffs with the help of overage juniors Bruno Baseotto and Bill Hobbins and the clutch goaltending of a young netminder by the name of Mike Vernon. Hobbins had been a large part of the Calgary team's success, leading the league in playoff scoring and approaching the junior loop's record for playoff scoring in a season. He would often team up with Baseotto on various scoring chances. On the eve of the upcoming Flames semi-final series the two helped engineer a come from behind 6-5 win in game four of their league final - Baseotto netting the game winning goal with only twenty seconds remaining on an excellent feed from Hobbins after a rink length rush into the Victoria defensive zone.

At the other end of the rink was Vernon, one of the smallest players on the ice. This Calgary born and raised goalie was emerging as one of the best goaltenders in Canadian junior hockey during the 1981 WHL playoffs. The Wranglers were the WHL Eastern Division champions after two rounds of playoff action. Calgary largely dominated a first round best of five series against the Lethbridge Broncos, that featured the likes of tenacious forwards, team captain Brent Sutter and brother Rich, in four games. Game four was Vernon's second shutout of the season and first of the playoffs. Then Vernon proved his worth against the Regina Pats who had come off a first round bye by virtue of their standing as the regular season Eastern Division leader. After a 5-0 drubbing in the first game at the hands of the Pats, Vernon and the entire Wranglers squad emerged as division champs under the leadership of coach Doug Sauter. Calgary was not expected by many WHL observers to win against a Pat lineup that featured three players with over 130 points including the WHL scoring champion Brian Varga.

The Regina lineup also featured future NHLer Garth Butcher who would go on to average better than two points per game versus Calgary in the Eastern final. This was Vernon's first season in the top level of Canadian junior hockey and as a result of playing well at the end of the regular season he became Sauter's choice for the netminding duties leaving Cam Sebastien as the backup during the playoffs.

Prior to the league final Calgary was not favoured to

win over the powerhouse Victoria, but as with the Flames the Wranglers were suddenly on the verge of greatness. Now here they were, Calgary was one win away from being on their way to a Memorial Cup appearance for the first time in 55 years. The Victoria Cougars had made short work of the Portland Winter Hawks in a four game sweep and showed their might scoring at will against an overmatched Portland franchise. They also had the number one goaltending prospect in Canada in net and believed to be the best junior hockey had to offer. He was an easy going eighteen year old from Spruce Grove, Alberta, a young man by the name of Grant Fuhr.

Fuhr had not been his absolute best against Calgary and the Wranglers fans hoped it would continue for at least one more victory to present itself. A WHL championship and a team in the Memorial Cup tournament along with an NHL team competing for the Stanley Cup, Calgary and the Corral were the hockey center of the universe.

The Minnesota North Stars were not concerned with the exploits of the junior Wranglers or the Flames for that matter. During the 1980 playoffs the North Stars emerged as a contender for the Stanley Cup having made it to the semi-finals before being beaten by the same Pat Quinn lead Philadelphia Flyers the Flames had encountered much trouble with this year. The North Stars drive for the cup in 1980 was very similar to the Flames drive this season, Minnesota being a good club, but had never truly done anything magical when it counted in the playoffs. Now these two teams were on a collision course.

The first game of this best of seven semi-final series would be played in the Corral due to Calgary's better regular season record. After their grueling series against the Flyers, the North Stars were a welcome competitor. For a number of Calgary fans the competition did not matter, all that did was the availability of tickets, which were in the form of a six game ticket package selling at $150 per package. Fans were lined up outside the Corral to get their chance to buy tickets to see their heroes in action. The sea of red had swept the city and the few unbelievers had jumped onboard. Talk of the Stanley Cup was beginning to excite the city and for the first time since the Calgary Tigers left by train for Montreal in 1924 that historic trophy looked to be in sight.

The Corral was once again the place to be on the night of Tuesday, April 28, 1981. The stand-in for a future as yet to be designed structure had done very well for the Flames in their first year in Calgary. With the quaintness of a small town rink combined with the sounds of rabid fans, the Corral was now becoming known as an intimidating place to play for NHL opponents. However, the Minnesota North Stars were a team that refused to be intimidated on the road. Over the course of the 1980 and 81 playoffs, going into the Calgary series, Minnesota had only lost three of fourteen games in their opponent's home barn. In the 1981 playoffs they were an amazing 5-0 on the road. So the myths about the Corral that had spread about the NHL would be of no concern to them.

While Calgary's NHL neighbours to the north, the Edmonton Oilers, were considered the youngest up and coming team in the league, Minnesota was certainly another. Due to a rash of injuries that cost the North Stars over 300 man games from its roster, the club suffered during the long regular season. However, this did allow the inclusion of younger players that might not have otherwise made the lineup. The North Stars had the likes of Neal Broten and Steve Christoff, members of the 1980 U.S. Olympic "Miracle on Ice" team. Another 1980 Olympian in the form of Canadian national team member Kevin Maxwell, a 20 year old forward, was making key contribution in defeating the Boston Bruins and Buffalo Sabres in the playoffs. There were also underage junior players such as Ken Solheim and Brad Palmer to add into the mix. Probably the best new addition of youth was a call-up from Minnesota's Oklahoma City farm team, Dino Ciccarelli.

Ciccarelli was a product of the London Knights of the Ontario junior league and had blossomed in his entry to the NHL during the second half of the regular season. He had been on a better than point per game pace with Oklahoma City of the Central Hockey League and earned his call to the big league quickly. Ciccarelli was on the small side at five feet ten inches tall and only 180 pounds, but proved he could take the pounding of the big leagues, dish out some hits to his opponents and score in the process. Unlike other talented snipers, Ciccarelli would not hear his name called during the draft and would sign with the team as a free agent. The media had dubbed the North Stars collection of youth as "the Kiddie Corps" however, Calgary felt that they could take these "kids" to school.

As soon as the puck dropped for game one it was clear that the North Star youngsters were flight of foot or in this case, flight of skate. The first period was showing that this would be a different series than the two previous. Speed and skill would be the dominant factors. End to end action had the 7000 plus Corral fans on the edge of their seats. From the beginning it appeared that Calgary's game plan was to have their defense come up with the forwards on rushes into the Minnesota defensive zone. In other words the Flames had turned into an even more aggressive team. This was largely the result of the stellar play of Pat Riggin throughout the Philadelphia series. A team with a goaltender playing well is very dangerous as confidence throughout the rest of the team grows. A defenseman might jump into a play he otherwise would not if playing conservatively. The thinking being, if I am caught up ice with my partner facing a two on one situation, our goalie will make the save and help me out for my error. This must have been the thinking for game one of the Minnesota series as Riggin would face several two on one and three on two situations plus an occasional breakaway in the first period and throughout the contest.

Phil Russell would draw a penalty at 13:08 of the first and with only seconds remaining young North Star defenseman Craig Hartsburg scored as Russell readied himself to step back on to the ice. It was 1-0 Minnesota going into the second frame. Other than the Hartsburg goal both Riggin and the North Stars Guy Meloche were holding the fort for their respective teams. However, one thing was becoming apparent, the North Stars were a fast skating team and much faster than had been previously anticipated. Their ability to turn one on one or two on two situations into a two on one or three on two would eventually open the game up and if Calgary could not counter it by tightening up defensively the Flames would be in trouble.

Minnesota had thwarted a couple Calgary power play opportunities in the first period, but the Flames vaunted power play could not slip the puck past the goal line. This was due to the excellent work of penalty killing forwards Kent Erik Andersson, Tim Young, Brad Palmer and Kevin Maxwell. They did very well in keeping Calgary's defense from getting excellent scoring opportunities from the points and clearing errant pucks from the North Star zone. Early in the second period Tim Young would score off a setup from Palmer to make it 2-0 North Stars only moments after a Calgary player had left the penalty box.

Jim Peplinski would respond for Calgary with less than five minutes to go in the second, cutting the Minnesota lead to 2-1. During this span of play Calgary's "Magic Man" was Kent Nilsson who would get a breakaway opportunity showing Calgary had speed to burn as well. Nilsson roared in on North Star goalkeeper Gilles Meloche, the flaming C on his chest bouncing about with each stride. Nilsson's eyes were focused alternating between the black disk on his stick and the green and yellow clad figure in front of a freshly painted bright red net. Nilsson looked to be moving to the right as his shoulders, arm and leg actions indicated such a move. Meloche was not buying it as he slowly slid back towards his net. Nilsson quickly shifted to his left, Meloche followed stretching his body out across the ice while stacking his goalie pads. Nilsson was looking at a largely wide open net with only Meloche's waving legs in the way. He drew back his Koho brand stick and let a wrist shot go towards the net. The crowd at the Corral began to rise up in excitement, waiting for the inevitable. A collection of groans filled the Corral rather than cheers, Kent Nilsson's shot had hit the post and the puck would tumble harmlessly away from the Minnesota net.

However, Minnesota kept coming and once again Tim Young was in on the action. With Brad Maxwell in the penalty box for a tripping minor, Young would manage to get a piece of the puck while Paul Reinhart attempted to clear it. The puck would come loose and Gordie Roberts would pick it up and send a pass up to teammate Young with Reinhart desperately trying to catch up. Young let a low shot loose on Riggin who made the initial save, but the short rebound sat on the ice long enough for Gord Roberts to get his stick on it and give Minnesota a 3-1 lead going into the second intermission.

The penalty killers struck again at the beginning of the third period, ironically on the same Brad Maxwell penalty. Once again Paul Reinhart was the last man back and he would have to contend with two fast North Star forwards once again. Once again Tim Young lead the charge into the Calgary end of the rink. Young stickhandled and began skating away from the Calgary net within the defensive zone. Pat Riggin focused on Young and Reinhart decided to make an attempt to check the puck from the North Star forward. It looked to be the correct play as Young was nearing the point of no return for a scoring chance. A few more strides and he would be behind the net, the only thought could be to shoot and Riggin had the angle covered. Young saw that Al MacAdam was in the clear, nearing the Flames net and he put a beautiful pass across towards him. All MacAdam had to do was put his stick on the puck and guide it into an empty net. Both Riggin and Reinhart had turned their heads just long enough to see MacAdam make a motion with his stick and see the red light go on behind them. It was 4-1 Minnesota, which would turn out to be the final score. Calgary was down one game in the series and had lost home ice advantage.

It had been clear the Flames were facing a much younger and faster club than the previous two series. Rather than dictating a strong physical defensive game that had been the key in the Flyer series, Calgary played Minnesota's wide open style. With all the odd man chance Calgary had given up to Minnesota the score could easily have been 8-1. Once again Pat Riggin had stood tall, but it was clear the Flames would need to change their style of play back to that of the Flyers series to have a chance to win.

The Flames were still very much in this series; unfortunately the other Calgary franchise enjoying success that spring, the junior Wranglers, would lose their best of seven final series to Victoria and a chance at winning the Memorial Cup, the symbol of supremacy in Canadian junior hockey. Victoria came roaring back to take the last three games in the series after being down three games to one, most of it due to the abilities of their goaltender. Grant Fuhr had won the first of what would be many pivotal engagements with hometown hero Mike Vernon. The Wranglers did have a great year and would be forced to join the rest of Calgary in watching hockey. However disappointed followers of the team were, the chance at the Stanley Cup was still at hand.

The last day of April 1981, a Thursday, would be the night for game two. It would be an aggressive and dominant Flames team that would entertain the Corral crowd of 7226. The Flames were revved up for game two. The team came out hitting and putting pressure on Minnesota's defense that was fast, but much smaller than the majority of Calgary's forwards. Al MacNeil and Pierre Page also came up with a system where Calgary's defense could keep pinching with some help from their centers. Calgary's coaching staff encouraged the left and right wingers to jump on the North Stars defensemen quickly, but instructed the centers to hang back when possible to assist the defensemen.

Calgary players executed and nine minutes would pass in the first period of game two before Minnesota would register their first shot on Pat Riggin who was once again the starting goalie. By that time Calgary was up 2-0 with Pekka Rautakallio scoring his first playoff marker on a Don Lever pass and Rautakallio sending a pass to Guy Chouinard to convert into a goal.

Calgary was dominant throughout the first and one

time Cleveland Baron, Gilles Meloche, was the busiest he had been thus far in the series. While the shots would end 13-9 in favour of Calgary for the first period, the shot clock showed how ineffective the shot clock can be at determining the balance of play. Several more Flames shots directed at Meloche missed by only inches outside the posts and these do not count in the totals. Time and time again Calgary could not convert on some inspired plays as pucks soared wide of the net. The first period was much more in the Flames favour than the shot clock would allow.

  The 2-0 Calgary lead held up through the second period and into the third - Riggin denying a glorious chance by Dino Ciccarelli on a breakaway and Meloche doing the same to Willi Plett at the other end of the rink during the second period. Minnesota had shown some fight in the second engaging in the aggressive tactics of the Flames. However, Calgary nearly put Minnesota away for good when the line of Don Lever, Chouinard and Ken Houston bumped their way into the North Stars defensive zone. Houston and Chouinard quickly threw passes across to each other then to Lever cruising along near the North Star net. With Gilles Meloche out of position, Lever need only throw the puck into an empty cage. The Corral fans were ready to once again celebrate, unfortunately Lever missed the net and a glorious opportunity to put game two to bed, and it was still 2-0 Calgary.

Calgary was now laying back in the third period simply trying to protect their two goal lead and ride out the last twenty minutes of the game out. Usually such a tactic gives an opening to the trailing team, this occasion would be no different. The time for dump and chase hockey had come as five white shirts with flaming Cs on their chests stood firm at the center ice line. Eventually, Minnesota's Kevin Giles would be left alone long enough to slap a pass from linemate Al MacAdam into the Flames net to cut the Flames lead to 2-1.

The Corral crowd was growing nervous, but the fans continued to shout and encourage their hockey heroes to keep going. North Star forward Tim Young, the hero of game one, was injured getting out of a scrum with Calgary's Jamie Hislop and Pekka Rautakallio. Young injured his knee on the play and had to be carried off the ice on a stretcher. It would be that type of game. Willi Plett and Ken Houston hit every North Star that was near them. Unfortunately, Plett drew four penalties from referee Dave Newell during the course of the game for his aggressive action.

Kevin Lavallee, who was doing very well in his first playoff season, scored his third goal of the post season to give the Flames another two goal lead. Then the North Stars struck back at 10:34 of the third on a goal by Steve Christoff, a power play goal with Plett looking on from the penalty box, his fourth time in the sin bin that night.

The score was now 3-2 Calgary and the final nine minutes would see close checking hockey the rest of the way. Fortunately, for the Flames, Minnesota ran out of time and the series would be even at one win each. As Pat Riggin, Bob Murdoch and the rest of the Flames stepped off the ice Calgary's quest for the Stanley Cup appeared to be on course.

Games three and four were scheduled for the North Stars home rink in Bloomington, Minnesota, a suburb of nearby Minneapolis. With the series tied at one game apiece, enthusiasm was high on both sides. A group of Calgarians even rented a Lear jet to make the trip to Minnesota to see their Flames get closer to the Stanley Cup. After the second game optimism was abundant and hockey fans across the nation were tuning in to see Canada's newest NHL franchise go on a remarkable run on CBC television.

Minnesota general manager Lou Nanne was quite content with a split in Calgary. He knew the best was yet to be seen from his young guns. While game two would be a setback Nanne and coach Glen Sonmor could see Calgary was a tired team especially after playing the emotional Flyers series. Nanne knew the North Stars could out hustle the Flames and this would bring many scoring opportunities to his young team. Could the Flames defense and goaltending withstand such an onslaught?

On May 3, 1981 the Flames struck first in game three of the series. Ken Houston would score a much needed goal that would keep the fans cheering back in Calgary and in Bloomington just past the three minute mark of the first period. However, the North Stars would strike back to make the score 2-1 Minnesota at the first intermission.

During the second frame the North Star and Flames changed leads twice and the score going into the third period was a 4-4 draw. Calgary took the play to the North Stars during the third period out shooting their opponent 12-5 in some frantic action. Then one of the North Star youngsters, Steve Christoff, made it 5-4 for the hometeam just over four minutes into the period. The Flames kept pressing hard, but Gilles Meloche was up to the challenge. Bobby Smith added an empty net goal to make the final score a 6-4 win for Minnesota. The Flames were now down two games to one.

While the score was close and the Flames had done very well in out chancing the North Stars, it was becoming clear that Minnesota's youthful skilled forwards were putting pressure on the Flames defense. Even young Brad Marsh had had problems knocking the first Minnesota goal in accidentally in game three, which was credited to Bobby Smith. Plus Calgary was missing star forward Kent Nilsson who was undergoing surgery to remove a small bone fragment from his shoulder.

Game four would show exactly how much youth and depth would play a factor in this series. Coach Sonmor decided to rest Gilles Meloche and gave the goaltending duties to nineteen year old Don Beaupre, an underage junior player from Kitchener, Ontario. Beaupre had done so well at the North Stars training camp that Lou Nanne decided to keep him with the big team rather than sending him back to another year of junior hockey with the Sudbury Wolves in northern Ontario. As a result Minnesota dealt Gary Edwards, the number two goalie, to Edmonton to make room for Beaupre. He did not disappoint, performing very well in net in tandem with Meloche throughout the regular season.

It would be Beaupre versus Al MacNeil's choice, Reggie Lemelin, in game four. This would be the night that Dino Ciccarelli would become a household name across Canada. Ciccarelli opened the scoring for Minnesota at 3:01 of the first period. Then Calgary answered six minutes later. Calgary began to show their fatigue and by the end of the first period it was 3-1 for the home squad. The shot clock showed Minnesota had peppered Lemelin with 19 shots while Calgary had only managed eight. Jaime Hislop cut the score to 3-2 then Ciccarelli took over. With his first goal earlier in the game Ciccarelli had tied the rookie record for goals in the Stanley Cup playoffs with eight. Ironically, the record holder was sitting on the bench with him, forward Steve Christoff who had set the record in Minnesota's 1980 playoff run. Then Ciccarelli popped in his ninth and tenth goals of the playoffs both on assists from linemates Tom McCarthy and Bobby Smith, shattering the previous rookie record. Now it was 5-2 and it would 6-2 Minnesota going into the third period. Calgary would add two more goals late in the game to make it a more respectable 7-4 North Star victory. However, the fans and players knew it was not even close. Calgary staged a late comeback, but it was too little too late. Unfortunately, Calgary was in a deep hole now down three games to one and heading back to the Corral for game six. To add insult to injury, the Pacific Western charter the Flames had rented to return to home had mechanical problems and would arrive around three o'clock in the morning. Surprisingly there were some Calgary fans waiting to encourage their heroes, which was becoming normal practice at Calgary International.

So there were the Calgary Flames, being forced to rise above and try to fight back as the Philadelphia Flyers had almost done to them, one of the ironies of playoff hockey. Minnesota had shown its youth, speed and skill in games three and four and the Flames made the mistake of trying to compete at that style of game. Banging and crashing plus making the best of opportunities presented was the style the Flames needed to win. It had been a massacre broadcasted across Canada. Suddenly some were wondering if their new darlings had gone too far in the playoffs. Being so close and falling so hard after a tremendous run might be too much. However, the Flames had other ideas.

If anything was going to turn this series around the much maligned Corral might help. While there was little being said to the media Calgary was a team that had gone to war with Philadelphia and was beginning to run out of gas. Coach MacNeil told reporters that the Minnesota victories were more a result of Calgary miscues than Minnesota opportunities. This may have been true for game three, but game four was a disaster. Even Pat Riggin had to come in to spell off Lemelin when the carnage continued.

When the Flames stepped out on to the Corral ice on the evening of May 7, 1981, the Corral erupted. The crowd was doing all it could to exhort its hockey icons on. As they whirled about on the ice the cheers became louder. The names that had thrilled a city for nearly a year, Clement, Houston, Marsh, Plett and the others raced about. The Calgary hockey fans were going to give back to the team what the team had given to them. Calgary was no longer just a frontier city on the edge of the Rockies or an oil city, it was now a hockey city and the Flames had done that for them.

Prior to the game the Flames had received encouragement from Nelson Skalbania who wrote on the blackboard in the team's dressing room that each player would get two tickets to Hawaii regardless of the outcome of the series. As well Boston Celtics head coach Bill Fitch sent the Flames management a telegram that was posted for the players. In it Fitch mentioned that he felt the Flames had the same qualities as the Bill Russell lead Celtics team had that overcame a three games to one deficit to the Philadelphia 76ers in a best of seven semi-final series from 1968. The Celtics then went on to win the National Basketball Association title. He saw no reason why the Flames could not do it as well. This also showed how much attention was being paid to this series, which was even greater now that the New York Islanders had swept the Rangers in four games and were now awaiting their opponent for the Stanley Cup final.

Game five would be a dogfight. Minnesota was once again dominant with their up tempo style and took the advantage in scoring chances and shots on goal. Pat Riggin once again rose to the occasion as the starting goalie making several spectacular saves throughout. The checking line of Willi Plett, Jim Peplinski and Randy Holt finally managed to bottle up the speedy Bobby Smith line with sniper Dino Ciccarelli riding shotgun. Calgary's power play also responded well early. Holt had been benched earlier and seemed to help give the Flames life in game five.

Bob MacMillan managed to break through with a

shot on Gilles Meloche, who had returned to the net even though Don Beaupre had performed well in game four, on a power play just as the first period was ending. With fans still returning to their seats MacMillan pumped another shot home to give Calgary a 2-0 lead before the first minute in the second period had passed by. The battles continued and the Calgary faithful did not breathe a sigh of relief until their blonde haired favourite, Willi Plett, scored to make it 3-0 early in the third period. Craig Hartsburg would finally respond for Minnesota, but it was too late. The Flames won 3-1 and the Calgary fans cheered wildly as the Flames stepped off the ice. Pat Riggin looked worn out after making 36 saves in this crucial game and Minnesota players praised Riggin's heroics following the game. Some observers felt Bobby Smith had taken a toll at the hands of Calgary's rough and tumble forwards. There was hope, as slim as it was, and Bloomington would once again be the location for the test. What Flames fans did not know was the words Bobby Smith had written on his game sticks, "Mental intensity, every shift, skate, defense, hit, move the puck". Hockey fans across Canada would learn this the next day in a report by the Canadian Press.

Game six would see the style of play open up more to Minnesota's liking. Minnesota took advantage of power play midway through the first frame to make it 1-0 early and give their fans an instant lift. Calgary struck with Willi Plett continuing his great playoff run with his eighth goal of the post-season to make it 1-1 early in the second period. Then Minnesota ran away from Calgary with three straight goals before Ken Houston could respond with about five minutes remaining in the game. Calgary and Minnesota would trade goals in the dying minutes before the game finished up as a 5-3 Minnesota win and Calgary's Cinderella run in the 1981 playoffs had finally come to an end. This had been the first time in four attempts that the North Stars had managed to get past the semi-finals, so it was a much deserved honour for this young team. However, the loss still hurt. As the Flames packed up to leave for home it was a bitter pill to swallow after all that they had done. A goal here, a penalty there, and they could have been the ones readying for a showdown with the defending champion Islanders.

After their flight touched down at Calgary International Airport, the players could see that a substantial crowd had formed by their arrival gate. Hundreds of Flames fans had shown up at the airport with signs and cheers wishing their heroes well. The Calgary Flames walked into the concourse at Calgary International as champions to their city, not losers. The players signed autographs, shook hands and slapped high fives. This truly showed the spirit of the people of Calgary and one homemade cardboard sign flapping above the heads of the crowd seemed to say it all. "Wait until next year!"

Index

Andersson, Kent Erik... 146
Barber, Bill... 115, 129, 138
Barkley, Doug... 81
Barris, Chuck.. 136
Beaupre, Don... 155
Bridegman, Mel... 115, 132
Browndridge, Bob... 33
Broten, Neil... 144
Butcher, Garth... 141
Bouchard, Dan... 53
Calgary, early settlement... 3-7
Calgary Corral... 23, 56, 69, 75, 76, 82, 89, 124, 142, 146
Calgary Cowboys... 37, 39
Calgary Wranglers... 140
Calgary Tigers... 18-20, 22
CFAC television... 81
Christoff, Steve... 144, 152, 155
Chouinard, Guy... 79, 85, 97, 100, 137
CHQR radio... 81
Ciccarelli, Dino... 144-145, 155
Clarke, Bobby... 127, 129
Clement, Bill... 49-50, 97
Cochrane, Glen... 132, 133
Cousins, Tom... 34, 46, 56, 62, 65, 66, 67
Craig, Jim... 47, 48
Creighton, Fred... 41
Currie, Frank... 24
Dailey, Bob... 111
Dionne, Marcel... 41, 42
Elbow River, skating rink... 9
Esposito, Tony... 91-92, 94, 96, 97
Finney, Sid... 24
Fletcher, Cliff... 34, 53, 76, 132
Fraser, George... 10
Ford, Glenn... 57-60

Ftorek, Robbie... 85
Fuhr, Grant... 142, 149
Geoffrion, Bernie... 35
Gorence, Tom... 116
Goulet, Michel... 86
Green, Norman... 69
Gregg, Randy... 98
Hartsburg, Craig... 146
Henderson, Paul... 74
Hislop, Jamie... 88, 116, 126, 152, 155
Hoggarth, Ron... 115
Holmgran, Paul... 111, 128, 130
Holt, Randy... 83
Horse Show Building... 16-17
Houston, Ken... 79, 88, 97, 116, 131, 137, 151, 152, 154, 157, 160
Hull, Bobby... 31-33, 37, 83
Ingarfield, Earl Jr.... 79
Irwin, George... 11
Kwong, Normie... 69
Labraaten, Dan... 95
Lafleur, Guy... 41, 42
Lavalle, Kevin... 138
Lemelin, Rejean... 91, 98, 101, 165, 155
Lever, Bob... 81
Linseman, Ken... 111, 123, 131, 133, 137
MacAdam, Al... 43-45, 77, 96, 148, 149, 152, 157
MacLeish, Rick.. 115
MacMillan, Bob... 79, 100
Magnusson, Kent... 99
Maher, Peter... 81
Maloche, Gilles... 147, 150, 154
Marsh, Brad... 72, 80, 92, 154
Marsh, Pete... 101
Maxwell, Kevin... 144, 146
Montreal Canadiens, early years... 20
Mulvey, Grant... 103

Murdoch, Bob... 80, 120, 126, 133
Nilsson, Kent... 79, 147
Orr, Bobby... 83
Page, Pierre... 77, 78, 150
Palmer, Brad... 144, 146
Peplinski, Jim... 79, 127, 132, 147
Peters, Pete... 116
Plett, Willi... 45, 72, 79, 86, 88, 89, 94, 99, 106, 112,115, 123, 125, 127, 128, 131, 132, 137, 139, 151, 132, 157, 158, 159
Poule, David... 77
Preston, Rich... 103
Propp, Brian.. 111, 134
Provonost, Jean... 78
Rautakallio, Pekka... 80, 150, 152
Reinhart, Paul... 76, 100, 133, 148
Richard, Henri... 43
Riggin, Pat... 82, 91, 116-117, 118, 120, 121-123, 131, 146, 158
Roberts, Gordie... 148
Ruskowski, Terry... 96
Russell, Phil... 95, 102, 128, 146
Quinn, Pat... 87, 110, 113, 116, 118, 125, 131, 142
St. Croix, Rick... 118, 120, 134
Stastny, Peter... 84, 86
Seaman, Byron... 56, 66, 67
Seaman, Daryl... 56, 61
Secord, Al... 96, 99
Sherman Rink... 11-13, 15
Sherman, W.B.... 12
Skalbania, Nelson... 61-65, 68, 119, 157
Smith, Bobby... 154, 156, 159
Stanley Cup, early years Calgary... 13, 14, 18-19
Sutter, Darryl... 95, 105
Turner, Lloyd... 13, 16-17, 18, 21
Unger, Gary... 72-73,75
Vail, Eric... 79
Van Hellemond, Andy... 85, 133, 134, 135

Van Horne, Jim... 92
Vancouver Maroons... 19
Vernon, Mike.. 140, 141, 149
Whalen, Ed... 82
Wilson, Behn... 111, 115
Wilson, Bert... 117, 130
Young, Tim... 146, 148
Ziegler, John... 38, 85